NTSE Mathematics

W o r k b o o k
C l a s s   V I I

A Mathematics Enrichment Workbook for Primary School Students

Chandan Sengupta

Creative Mathematics Series

NTSE Mathematics Workbook Class VII

A Mathematics Enrichment Workbook for Primary School Students.

Chandan Sengupta

This volume of publication is a part of Continuing Education Series. It is expected that this publication will address different nedd based involvement of fellow aspirants in their regular studies. Tere are worksheets from different ladders of studies to fulfill the objective of extending support to self propelled pace of learning..

Most of the worksheets are from regular classroom studies. Some of the worksheets are from Olympiads and other challenging examinations. We always keep a balance between higher order challenges and lower order assignments. It will enhance the participatory skill of the fellow student and also build up the competency pattern required for gaining mastery in mathematics. All practice and guidance efforts should be guided. That is why answers are not incorporated with this volume. There is a separate volume having all the answers and other needful assistance for teachers.

We can use some standard technique to correlate the memory and skill related to mathematical operations for facilitating proper and timely linkage of previous foundation with those of newly developed skill formation. We can use the worksheets and activities given in this workbook for providing an additional exposure to fellow students. Mixture of content areas will make it easy for the fellow student to grasp through it easily. Normal confluence of such practice session will also seed up the pace of learning.

This book is dedicated to fellow aspirants of Coontinuing Studies.

Contents

CONTENTS

Foreword

This workbook is designed to enhance the competencies of fellow students through allowing them to enhance their skills through extended practices. All the problems duly incorporated in this collection are of such type that they create an interest of learning in them. They make themselves absolutely fit for taking different higher challenges.

Geneeral mathematics is a subject area through which a student exposes oneself to other spheres of the correlated content areas of the curriculum. This collection is primarily meant for students of grade four of most of the balanced curriculum we have in our different boards. It can be considered more suitable for aspirants having affinity to opt for some higher challenges. One can even consider this collection for Olympiads and various other foundation courses. This workbook contains some activity sheets and reference worksheets suitable for the students of Grade 4. It is also suitable for aspirants preparing for Olympiads and other such enrichment activities.

Answer sheets with explanations are there in a separate booklet. It will enable parents and teachers for organizing the task in a better way. I am confident enough about the competence of fellow students having willingness to move up to the final stage of the Mathematics Enrichment Activities of various stages. There are different worksheets in accord to the time of studies that can be assigned to the fellow student. Answers are in a separate sheet paper that can be kept at different place. Parents and teachers use this book of activities to develop interest of students on mathematical as well as analytical skills.

Most of the calculations duly involved in these activities are of common types. One can do it with a little bit easiness. It is expected that students may enrich their knowledge base by following different worksheets and instructional materials with their respective acceleration of the pace of learning. They also need a timely guidance from their faculty members to go on experimenting. Enhancement of mathematical skills is the subject of timely practice. It should be planned regularly. Some of the question may come in different worksheets; it is done to ensure guided practice of selected portions of the workbook with better feedback. Repeating a portion of the guided instruction is most important and moving through new portions of the curriculum is obligatory. It is too easy to solve any mathematical problems with basic understanding; but it is too difficult to memorise all the mathematical problems with their operational steps. We also expect a kind of active participation from fellow aspirants for ensuring their timelt ascertained enhancement of skills and competencies. We are also optimistic to move on through different sections of the curriculum duly prescribed by different boards of studies. Central core of the curriculum is designed basically by Central Board of Secondary Education and

Research and Training (NCERT). That curriculum framework is our core of the entire design with which worksheets are presented. Mixing and inter-mixing of different portions of curriculum is made to ensure scheduled practice throughout the calendar of annual curriculum.

The core of the curriculum represents the format of most of the school curriculum we have in practice at different boards. Most of the parts are from School level formats of general types.

Main topics incorporated in this practice book are as follows:

1. Understanding numbers in their standard form and expanded form.

2. Decimals and fractions.

3. Ratio, proportion and percentage.

4. Everyday mathematics.

5. Divisibility rules, factors, multiples and prime numbers.

6. Lines, rays, line segments , angles and basic shapes.

7. Data handling, bar graphs, pie charts.

8. Measurements: Length, outer boundaries and areas.

9. General Understanding of Baisc Shapes and three dimensional objects.

10. Inter-conversion of decimals, fractions and percentage.

11. Problem solving abilities.

Chandan Sukumar Sengupta

Author

System of Numeration

Numbers having a definite position on a number line are considered as Rational Numbers. Such numbers can be represented in the form of a fraction having a non-zero natural number as a denominator.

1: 2 tenths = $2 \times \frac{1}{10}$; 2 hundredths = $2 \times \frac{1}{100}$; 2 thousandths = $2 \times \frac{1}{1000}$; 2 ten thousandths = $2 \times \frac{1}{10000}$

Write the following in standard form:

A: $\frac{1}{10} + \frac{11}{100} + \frac{111}{1000} + \frac{1101}{10000} + 121 =$ ....

B: $\frac{21}{10} + \frac{221}{100} + \frac{333}{1000} + \frac{4353}{10000} +$ $2021 =$ ....

2: Simplify:

a) $\left(1 + \frac{1}{2}\right)\left(1 + \frac{1}{3}\right)\left(1 + \frac{1}{4}\right) \dots \dots \dots \left(1 + \frac{1}{10,000}\right) X \left(1 - \frac{1}{10,001}\right) X\ 1{,}250\ = 5^p \times 10^q$; p = ...; q = ...;

b) 32 tens + 132 hundreds + 20 thousands + 21 thousandths + 102 hundredths + 1001 tenths = ...

3: Try to observe the following number pattern and complete the given steps.

$(1 + 3 + 5)$	=	3×3	=	3^2	=	9;
$(1 + 3 + 5 + 7 + 9 + 11)$	=	6×6	=	6^2	=	....;
(Sum of 11 consecutive odd numbers)	=	... X	=	$....^2$	=	121;
(Sum of 111 consecutive odd numbers)	=	.... X	=	$.....^2$	=	.......;
(Sum of 1111 consecutive odd numbers)	=	..... X	=	$.....^2$	=	........;

4: 48. $[1 X\ (1{,}001)^{-1} + 2X\ (1{,}001)^{-1} + 3X\ (1{,}001)^{-1} +$ ..... $1{,}000\ X\ (1{,}001)^{-1}\ ] \times 125{,}000{,}000\ =$ ....

[Express your answer in exponential form.]

5. If the angles $(2a - 10)^0$ and $(a - 11)^0$ are complementary, what is the value of 'a'?

6. Age of Fontana is 5 years less than Snehal. Five years back difference of their age was 10 years. Find sum total of their ages after five years.

7. Ratio of angles of a quadrilateral is 2:3:4:6. Find magnitude of all the angles.

8. What least number should be subtracted from seven digit greatest number to make the value divisible exactly by 22?

9. Sum total of 16,000 consecutive numbers starting from 1 is divided by 10,001 and then the value is multiplied by 8,000. Represent the result in exponential form.

Let us Revise

Rational numbers between 3 and 4 ...

$$q_1 = \frac{3+4}{2} = \frac{7}{2}; \quad 3 < \frac{7}{2} < 4$$

$$q_2 = \frac{3+\frac{7}{2}}{2} = \frac{\frac{13}{2}}{2} = \frac{13}{4}; \quad 3 < \frac{13}{4} < \frac{7}{2} < 4$$

$$q_3 = \frac{4+\frac{7}{2}}{2} = \frac{\frac{15}{2}}{2} = \frac{15}{4}; \quad 3 < \frac{13}{4} < \frac{7}{2} < \frac{15}{4} < 4$$

$$q_4 = \frac{\frac{7}{2}+\frac{13}{4}}{2} = \frac{\frac{14+13}{4}}{2} = \frac{\frac{27}{4}}{2} = \frac{27}{8};$$

$$3 < \frac{13}{4} < \frac{27}{8} < \frac{7}{2} < \frac{15}{4} < 4$$

$$q_5 = \frac{1}{2}\left(\frac{7}{2}+\frac{15}{4}\right) = \frac{1}{2}\left(\frac{14+15}{4}\right) = \frac{29}{8};$$

$$3 < \frac{13}{4} < \frac{27}{8} < \frac{7}{2} < \frac{29}{8} < \frac{15}{4} < 4$$

$$q_6 = \frac{1}{2}\left(\frac{13}{4}+\frac{27}{8}\right) = \frac{1}{2}\left(\frac{26+27}{8}\right) = \frac{53}{16};$$

$$3 < \frac{13}{4} < \frac{53}{16} < \frac{27}{8} < \frac{7}{2} < \frac{29}{8} < \frac{15}{4} < 4$$

$$\frac{7}{2}, \frac{13}{4}, \frac{15}{4}, \frac{27}{8}, \frac{29}{8} \text{ and } \frac{53}{16}.$$

1: Find out five rational numbers in between

a) 4 and 5.
b) 2 and 2.9
c) 1.001 and 1.002
d)

2: State whether the following statements are true or false. Give reasons for your answers.
(i) Every natural number is a whole number.
(ii) Every integer is a whole number.
(iii) Every rational number is a whole number.
(iv) Every irrational number is a real number.
(v) Every point on the number line is of the form $\sqrt{m}$, where m is a natural number.
(vi) Every real number is an irrational number.

3: Is zero a rational number?

4: Is it possible to work out a definite position on the number line for 2.009?

5. all rational numbers and all irrational numbers form the group (collection) of .... numbers.

6. Find whether following expressions have terminating or non-terminating types of decimals.

(i) $\frac{36}{100}$ (ii) $\frac{1}{11}$ (iii) $4\frac{1}{8}$ (iv) $\frac{3}{13}$ (v) $\frac{2}{11}$ (vi) $\frac{329}{400}$

7. You know that $\frac{1}{7} = 0.14\overline{2}857$. Predict what the decimal expansions of

$$\frac{1}{7}, \frac{3}{7}, \frac{4}{7}, \frac{5}{7}, \frac{13}{7}$$

8. Simplify: (1.111.... + 2.222.... + 3.333... + 4.444...) = ...

9. (3.333... X 5.5555.... X 7.777...) = ...

Revision 1

$$\frac{3}{2} = \frac{3 \times 5}{2 \times 5} = \frac{15}{10} = 1.5 \qquad [\text{Denominator} = 2 = 2^1]$$

$$\frac{1}{5} = \frac{1 \times 2}{5 \times 2} = \frac{2}{10} = 0.2 \qquad [\text{Denominator} = 5 = 5^1]$$

$$\frac{7}{8} = \frac{7 \times 125}{8 \times 125} = \frac{875}{1000} = 0.875$$
$$[\text{Denominator} = 8 = 2^3]$$

$$\frac{8}{125} = \frac{8 \times 8}{125 \times 8} = \frac{64}{1000} = 0.064$$
$$[\text{Denominator} = 125 = 5^3]$$

$$\frac{13}{20} = \frac{13 \times 5}{20 \times 5} = \frac{65}{100} = 0.65$$
$$[\text{Denominator} = 20 = 2^2 \times 5^1]$$

$$\frac{17}{16} = \frac{17 \times 625}{16 \times 625} = \frac{10625}{10000} = 1.0625$$
$$[\text{Denominator} = 16 = 2^4]$$

Q 1. What can be concluded by observing the given patterns of rational numbers?

Hints: The prime factorisation of q (i.e. denominator) has only powers of 2 or powers of 5 or powers of both.

Q2 . Give three examples of non-recurring non-terminating types of decimals.

Hints: square root of 2, 3 and 5 expressed in terms of decimal.

Q 3. Find the product of 1.333.... X 1.2222....

Q 4. Simplify: (0.9999 ..... X 0.222....) / 0.110110.....

Q 5. Simplify the following expression:

$$(1 + 2 + 3 + \dots + 1{,}000) \times \left(1 - \frac{1}{1001}\right) \times 25{,}000 \times 12{,}500 = (5)^p \times (10)^q. \quad p = \dots \quad q = \dots$$

[Ans: p = 8; q = 5]

Q 6. Reciprocal of a rational number is 1.5. Find fifth square of that rational number.   [32/243]

Q 7. $2/5^{th}$ of $15/23^{rd}$ of 690.069 + $11/19^{th}$ of 570.057 = ...X 300.003;   [Ans: 17]

Q 8. Three irrational numbers between $0.\ddot{7}\ddot{1}$ and $0.\ddot{8}\ddot{1}$ are

(i) 0.750750075000 .....   (ii) 0.767076700767000 ...... (iii) 0.78080078008000 ......

Similarly find out four irrational numbers in between 0.333...... and 0.4444.....

Q 9. Which of the following is not a rational number?

a) $\sqrt{23}$ b) $\sqrt{6.25}$ c) $\sqrt[3]{1331}$ d) $\sqrt[5]{0.00032}$ e) $(\sqrt{11 + \sqrt{20}} \times \sqrt{11 - \sqrt{20}})$

[Ans: Option a; Since square root of 23 is not a perfect square]

Q 10. Simplify: $(\sqrt{121 + 10\sqrt{42}} \times \sqrt{121 - 10\sqrt{42}}) \times 0.0079 \times \left(1 + \frac{1}{79}\right) \times \frac{50}{158} \times \frac{100}{316} = 10^{\,p}\dots$

[Ans: p = 5]

Q 11. What least number should be subtracted from 1341 X 10^{-6} to make the value exactly a cube?

[Ans : 10]

Q 12. Sum total of five rational numbers placed at an interval of 0.5 on a number line is equal to 10. Find product of the greatest and smallest rational numbers.

[Ans: 3.5]

Revision 2

I: Answer the following….

1: How many times do digits 3 occur if we write all the numbers from 1 to 100?

2. $(2.005 \times 20.05 \times 200.5 \times 2,005 \times 0.02005) \times 2005^{-1} \times 10^{-3} =$ ……….

3. Three fifth of ten eleventh of 33,077 =……………;   4. Half of a quarter of x = 16,096. X = ………

5. $\frac{1}{2} X \frac{2}{3} X \frac{3}{4} \dots\dots\dots\dots X \left(1 - \frac{1}{1000}\right) =$ …….

6. $\left(1 + \frac{1}{10}\right)\left(1 + \frac{1}{11}\right) \dots\dots\dots \left(1 + \frac{1}{10,001}\right) =$ ………

7. 20% of 60% of 100,400,600 = …….

8. $(2.345 + 23.45 + 234.5 + 2345) =$ ………

9. A comet passed by the Earth in the year 1835. It passes by the Earth every 60 years. Based on this information, in which of the following years can the comet be expected to pass by the Earth?

10. Somerfield can finish a project work in 16 days and his counterpart takes 24 days to finish the same project work. If they start working together then the project work can be finished in ……. Days.

11. Relationship of Celsius and Fahrenheit temperature scale is given by an equation on the basis of the fundamental intervals. Fundamental interval in Celsius scale is 1 and in Fahrenheit scale is 1.8.
(i) If the temperature is 86°F, what is the temperature in Celsius?
(ii) If the temperature is 35°C, what is the temperature in Fahrenheit?
(iii) If the temperature is 0°C what is the temperature in Fahrenheit and if the temperature is 0°F, what is the temperature in Celsius?
(iv) What is the numerical value of the temperature which is same in both the scales?

12. How many multiples of 22 located in between 100 and 200 are also multiples of 33?

13. Find out a greatest possible number of six digits which can be divided by 18, 36, 54 and 72 leaving remainder 17 in each case.

14. A wall mount clock strikes 5 bells at 5 O'Clock in 10 seconds. Calculate the time taken by this clock to strike 9 bells at 9 a.m.

15. What fraction of all the numbers from 1 to 100 are multiples of 11?

16. Simplify: $(3.333\dots + 4.44444\dots + 5.5555\dots) - (12.101010\dots) + \frac{1}{3} + \frac{1}{5} + \frac{1}{9}$

17. $\left(p + \frac{1}{p}\right) = 2;\ find\ the\ value\ of\ \left(p^2 - \frac{1}{p^2}\right)\left(p^2 + \frac{1}{p^2}\right)\left(p^4 + \frac{1}{p^4}\right)$

18. There is an increase of 36^0 F of temperature during day time in a city. Find the corresponding increase recorded in ^{0} C.

19. What least number should be subtracted from 120,903,807 to make the number divisible by 44?

20. While climbing a mountain the speed of Tenzing was 2 km per hour. During climbing down the speed was 6 km per hour. What time is spent by the climber for the expedition journey if height of the mountain is estimated as 2.25 km from the base camp?

Revision 3

I. Solve the following...

1. 0.46 _?_ 0.39   **2.** 0.709 _?_ 0.921   **3.** 0.06 _?_ 0.60

4. 9.8 _?_ 9.80   **5.** 0.509 _?_ 0.510   **6.** 0.623 _?_ 0.627

7. 0.4286 _?_ 0.4190   **8.** 0.5691 _?_ 0.5690   **9.** 0.53 _?_ 0.536

10. 0.8 _?_ 0.78   **11.** 7.610 _?_ 7.61   **12.** 7.3 _?_ 7.301

13. 2.34 _?_ 2.3513   **14.** 91.42 _?_ 90.425   **15.** 0.059 _?_ 0.59

Write in order from greatest to least.

16. 0.75, 0.39, 0.2, 0.35

17. 0.484, 0.495, 0.523, 0.54

18. 8.63, 8.6, 8.65, 7.99

19. 9.21, 9.0, 9.2, 9.06

20. 0.5478, 0.546, 0.5462, 0.5593

21. 8.134, 8.215, 8.2152, 8.2052

Write in order from least to greatest.

22. 2.7054, 0.9832, 1.2396, 0.9276

23. 2.7993, 0.0803, 0.0779, 0.2396

24. 21 thousandths, 201 hundredths, 2001 tenths, 12 hundredths, 102 tens, 12.9 ones

25. 1.001×10^5 , 10.01×10^6 , 100.1×10^7 , 1001×10^4 , 0.1001×10^6 , 100100×10^9

II. **Round to the nearest cent.**

1. \$4.368   **2.** \$5.472   **3.** \$35.476   **4.** \$12.525

5. \$.463   **6.** \$.085   **7.** \$1.5971   **8.** \$99.9943

Round each number to the underlined place.

9. 9<u>4</u>,329   **10.** 1<u>7</u>,721   **11.** 0.1<u>9</u>716   **12.** 3.14<u>1</u>59

13. 2.71<u>8</u>28   **14.** 10<u>0</u>.5003   **15.** 9<u>9</u>.59   **16.** 0.66<u>6</u>66

Round each number in the table to its greatest place.

17.

Ocean	Average Depth (feet)
Pacific	12,925
Atlantic	11,730
Indian	12,598
Arctic	3,407

18.

Continent	Area in Square Miles
Europe	3,800,000
Asia	17,200,000
Africa	11,700,000
Australia	3,071,000

III. Estimate the sum or difference. Use front-end estimation with adjustments.

1. $\quad$ 31.6 $\underline{+\,18.1}$	**2.** $\quad$ 68.7 $\underline{-\,63.9}$	**3.** $\quad$ 7.5 $\underline{-\,2.9}$	**4.** $\quad$ 9.1 $\underline{-\,3.6}$	**5.** $\quad$ 0.87 $\underline{-\,0.54}$
6. $\quad$ 0.74 $\underline{-\,0.15}$	**7.** $\quad$ 76.67 23.89 $\underline{+\,69.47}$	**8.** $\quad$ 16.34 44.59 $\underline{+\,39.07}$	**9.** $\quad$ 0.66 0.7 $\underline{+\,0.19}$	**10.** $\quad$ 0.84 0.59 $\underline{+\,0.8}$

Estimate the sum or difference by rounding.

11. $\quad$ 18.1534 $\underline{+\quad 7.0901}$	**12.** $\quad$ 4.8359 $\underline{-\,0.7473}$	**13.** $\quad$ 0.45601 $\underline{+\,0.06428}$	**14.** $\quad$ 4371.5902 $\underline{-\quad 127.3246}$
15. $\quad$ 386,002,444 $\underline{-\quad 49,624,973}$	**16.** $\quad$ 2.361912 $\underline{-\,0.19008}$	**17.** $\quad$ 952.0667 232.608 $\underline{+\,351.03991}$	**18.** $\quad$ 7.30267 45.37 $\underline{+\quad 0.84652}$

19. $(1 + 2 + 3 + \ldots\ldots 1000) \times (1001)^{-1} \times 500 = 5^p \times 10^q$; p = ... ; q = ...;

20. $(10{,}001 + 101{,}101 + 1101100 + 10{,}11{,}001) - (20{,}002 + 101{,}101) =$ ....

21. $(10 + 10 + 10 + \ldots\ldots 1000 \text{ times}) \times 10^{-1}\, 1001^{-1} \times 2500 = a^b$; a = ... ; b = ...;

IV. Estimate using rounding. Then find the sum.

1. $\quad$ 7 $\underline{+\,8.56}$	**2.** $\quad$ 6.4922 $\underline{+\quad 15.58}$	**3.** $\quad$ \$11,873.52 $\underline{+\quad 4,906.09}$	**4.** $\quad$ 2,527,004,609 $\underline{+\quad 38,211,073}$
5. $\quad$ 3,465,892 $\underline{+\,2,396,087}$	**6.** $\quad$ 1.6902333 $\underline{+\,0.7197807}$	**7.** $\quad$ 526,381,485 $\underline{+\,574,626,009}$	**8.** $\quad$ 3,245,840,900 $\underline{+\quad 80,059,275}$

9. $3.905 + 4.96$ $\qquad$ 10. $0.4791 + 1.085$ $\qquad$ 11. $0.10907 + 0.092$

12. $0.2613 + 0.45 + 0.852$ $\qquad$ 13. $0.5441 + 9.3 + 0.4637$

14. $567{,}074 + 96{,}132 + 8650$ $\qquad$ 15. $9{,}732{,}785 + 13{,}820{,}465$

Choose the correct addends for each sum. Use estimation to help you.
Explain in your Math Journal the method you used for each exercise.

	Sum	Addends			
16.	6.0108	0.6	4.321	2.1408	3.27
17.	1.4868	0.814	0.143	0.6293	0.7145

Rationals and Polynomials

Rational Numbers….

Now the rational numbers between $\dfrac{50}{100}$ and $\dfrac{90}{100}$ are

$$\dfrac{5}{10} = \dfrac{50}{100} < \dfrac{51}{100} < \dfrac{52}{100} < \dfrac{53}{100} < \ldots < \dfrac{89}{100} < \dfrac{90}{100} = \dfrac{9}{10}$$

Similarly, when we consider

$$\dfrac{5}{10} = \dfrac{500}{1000} \quad \text{and} \quad \dfrac{9}{10} = \dfrac{900}{1000}$$

So $\dfrac{5}{10} = \dfrac{500}{1000} < \dfrac{501}{1000} < \dfrac{502}{1000} < \dfrac{503}{1000} < \ldots < \dfrac{899}{1000} < \dfrac{900}{1000} = \dfrac{9}{10}$

The set of digits which repeats in non-terminating recurring decimal is called period.

For example

In $0.3333 \ldots = 0.\overline{3}$ the period is 3

In $0.12757575 \ldots = 0.12\overline{75}$ the period is 75

The number of digits in a period of non-terminating recurring decimal is called periodicity.

For example

In $0.3333 \ldots = 0.\overline{3}$ the periodicity is 1

In $0.12757575 \ldots = 0.12\overline{75}$ the periodicity is 2

The period of $0.23143143143\ldots =$ ________ periodicity = ________

The period of $125.6788989 \ldots =$ ________ periodicity = ________

I: Categorise the following as terminating and non-terminating decimals:
a) 1/11th of 1.01   b) 3/7th of 7,007   c) 1/9th of 11.011   d) 2/5th of 121.121

e) 1/9th of 1/7th of 93.163   f) 5th multiple of 1/3rd of fourth multiple of 0.125

Some examples to show rationalisation of repeated decimals:

Express each of the following decimals in rational forms i) $0.\overline{54}$ ii) $4.\overline{7}$

$0.\overline{54}$

let $x = 0.\overline{54}$

$\Rightarrow x = 0.545454....$ ------------------ (i)

here the periodicity of the decimal is two.

So we multiply both sides of (i) by 100, we get

$100x = 54.5454....$ ------------------ (ii)

On subtracting (ii) – (i)

$100x = 54.5454$ ......

$\underline{x = 0.5454 \text{ .....}}$

$\underline{99x = 54.0000......}$

$x = \dfrac{54}{99}$. Hence $0.\overline{54} = \dfrac{54}{99}$.

$4.\overline{7}$

let $x = 4.\overline{7}$

$x = 4.777....$ ---------------- (i)

here the periodicity of the decimal is one.

So multiply both sides of (i) by 10, we get

$10x = 47.777....$ ---------------- (ii)

Subtracting (i) from (ii) we get

$10x = 47.777$ .....

$\underline{x = 4.777 \text{ .....}}$

$\underline{9x = 43.0}$

$x = \dfrac{43}{9}$ Hence $4.\overline{7} = \dfrac{43}{9}$

1. Express each of the following in the form of p/q.

   a) 1.001   b) 8.125   c) 11.1111....   d) 121.232323........

2. Express each of the following decimals in the rational form.

   (i) $0.\overline{9}$ (ii) $0.\overline{57}$ (iii) $0.7\overline{29}$ (iv) $12.2\overline{8}$ (v) $0.\overline{9} + 0.\overline{9}$ ...... 81 times

3. Find $(x + y) \div (x - y)$ if

   (i) $x = \dfrac{5}{2},\ y = -\dfrac{3}{4}$ (ii) $x = \dfrac{1}{4},\ y = \dfrac{3}{2}$

4. Divide the sum of $-\dfrac{13}{5}$ and $\dfrac{12}{7}$ by the product of $-\dfrac{13}{7}$ and $-\dfrac{1}{2}$.

5. If $\dfrac{2}{5}$ of a number exceeds $\dfrac{1}{7}$ of the same number by 36. Find the number.

6. Two pieces of lengths $2\dfrac{3}{5}$ m and $3\dfrac{3}{10}$ m are cut off from a rope 11 m long. What is the length of the remaining rope?

7. The cost of $7\dfrac{2}{3}$ meters of cloth is ₹ $12\dfrac{3}{4}$. Find the cost per metre.

Guided Practice A

Let us study an example:

Sum of two numbers is 29 and one number exceeds another by 5. Find the numbers.

We have a puzzle here. We don't know the numbers. We have to find them.

Let the smaller number be 'x', then the bigger number will be '$x + 5$'.

But it is given that sum of these two numbers is 29

$\Rightarrow x + x + 5 = 29$

$\Rightarrow \quad 2x + 5 = 29$

$\therefore \quad 2x = 29 - 5$

$\therefore \quad 2x = 24$

$x = \dfrac{24}{2} \quad$ (Transposing '2' to RHS)

$x = 12.$

Second example:

Four times a number reduced by 5 equals 19. Find the number.

If the number is taken to be 'x'

Then four times of the number is '$4x$'

When it is reduced by 5 it equals to 19

$\Rightarrow \quad 4x - 5 = 19$

$4x = 19 + 5 \qquad$ (Transposing -5 to RHS)

$4x = 24$

$\therefore x = \dfrac{24}{4} \qquad$ (Transposing 4 to RHS)

$\Rightarrow x = 6$

Hence the required number is 6

1: Solve the following:

a) 21 times a number exceeds 147th multiple of six digit smallest number by 42. Find the number.

b) Sum total of two digits of a three digit number is 6. Digit at tens position is zero. If digits of ones place and tens place are inter-exchanged then the number obtained is 396 greater than the given number. Find the given number.

c) The length of a rectangular park exceeds its breadth by 17 meters.   If perimeter of that park is 178 meters find dimensions and area of the park.

d) Two angles supplementary to each other differ by 54^0. Find the angles.

e) Three angles of a triangle are in the ratio of 1: 2: 3. Find the smallest angle.

f) Sum total of eleven consecutive multiples of a number exceeds eleventh multiple of six digit smallest number by 66. Find smallest and greatest number of that number series.

Example: There are 90 multiple choice questions in a test. Two marks are awarded for every correct answer and one mark is deducted for every wrong answer . If Sahana got 60 marks in the test while she answered all the questions, then how many questions did she answer correctly?

Solution: Suppose the number of correctly answered questions be 'x', then number of wrongly answer questions $= 90 - x$.

It is given that for every correct answer 2 marks are awarded.

$\therefore$ Number of marks scored for correct answers $= 2x$

And it is given that for every wrongly answered questions '1' mark is deducted

$\therefore$ Number of marks to be deducted from the score

$$= (90 - x) \times 1 = 90 - x$$

Total score $= 2x - (90 - x) = 2x - 90 + x = 3x - 90$

But it is given that total score is 60

$$\Rightarrow \quad 3x - 90 = 60$$
$$3x = 60 + 90$$
$$3x = 60 + 90$$
$$3x = 150$$
$$x = \frac{150}{3} = 50$$

Number of questions answered correctly $= x = 50$

2. Ravi works as a cashier in a bank. He has currency of denominations ₹ 100, ₹ 50, ₹ 10 respectively. The ratio of number of these notes is 2 : 3 : 5. The total cash with Ravi is ₹ 4,00,000.

3. Find 'x' in the following figures?

(i)

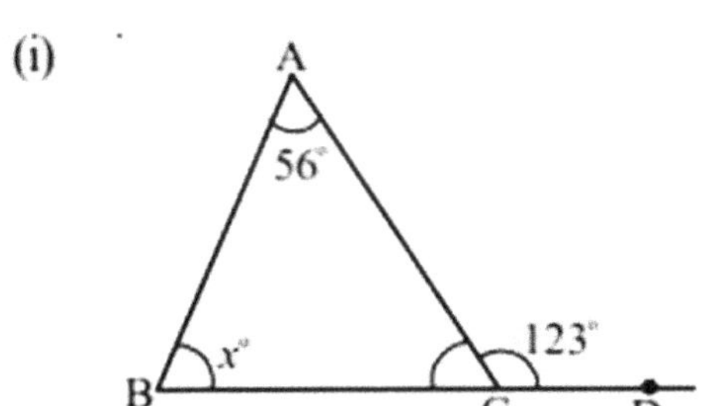

(ii)

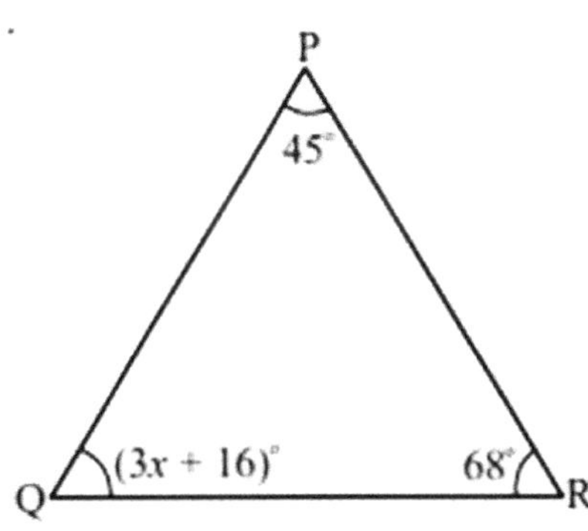

(iii)

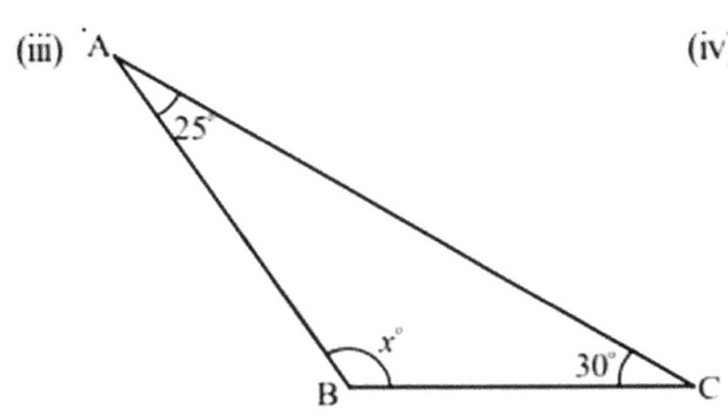

(iv)

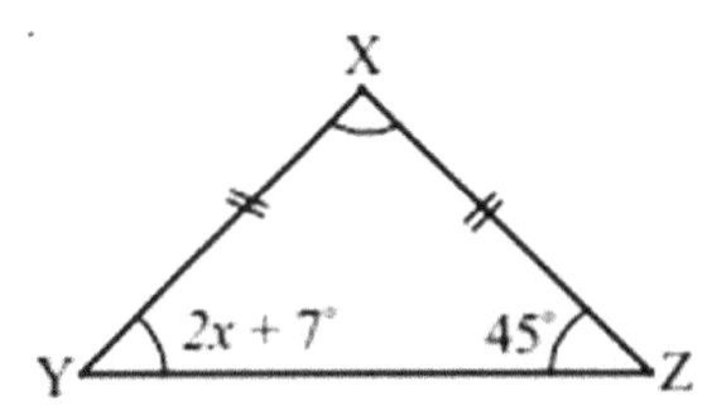

(v)

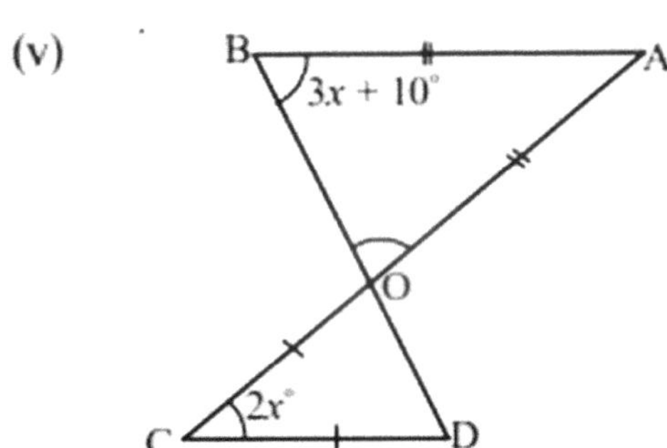

4. A two digit number exceeds its reciprocal by 49.08. Find the number.

5. What fraction of sum total of three consecutive multiples of a number 194 becomes 4th multiple of 17 if 29 added to it?

6: Sum total of four consecutive number exceeds fourth multiple of six digit smallest number by 10. Find the numbers.

7: After adding 1 to a number we get another number p. after subtracting 1 from the same number we get another number q. Product of p and q becomes 9,999. By using identities find out the number. If that number is considered as x then find out the folloing expression.

$$x^6 + x^5 + x^4 + x^3 + x^2 + x^1 + x^0 + x^{-1} + x^{-2} + x^{-3} + x^{-4}$$

8: Find value of p in the following expression.

$[(1.008 + 1.008 + \ldots\ldots 3{,}000 \text{ times}) - (0.0024 + 0.0024 + 0.0024 \ldots\ldots 10{,}000 \text{ times})] \times 9 = p^3.$

Guided Practce B

Solve the following equations:

1. $7x - 5 = 2x$

2. $5x - 12 = 2x - 6$

3. $7p - 3 = 3p + 8$

4. $8m + 9 = 7m + 8$

5. $7z + 13 = 2z + 4$

6. $9y + 5 = 15y - 1$

7. $3x + 4 = 5(x-2)$

8. $3(t - 3) = 5(2t - 1)$

9. $5(p - 3) = 3(p - 2)$

10. $5(z + 3) = 4(2z + 1)$

11. $15(x - 1) + 4(x + 3) = 2(7 + x)$

12. $3(5z - 7) + 2(9z - 11) = 4(8z - 7) - 111$

13. $8(x - 3) - (6 - 2x) = 2(x + 2) - 5(5 - x)$

14. $3(n - 4) + 2(4n - 5) = 5(n + 2) + 16$

II. Solve the following equations.

(i) $\dfrac{n}{5} - \dfrac{5}{7} = \dfrac{2}{3}$

(ii) $\dfrac{x}{3} - \dfrac{x}{4} = 14$

(ii) $\dfrac{z}{2} + \dfrac{z}{3} - \dfrac{z}{6} = 8$

(iv) $\dfrac{2p}{3} - \dfrac{p}{5} = 11\dfrac{2}{3}$

(v) $9\dfrac{1}{4} = y - 1\dfrac{1}{3}$

(vi) $\dfrac{x}{2} - \dfrac{4}{5} + \dfrac{x}{5} + \dfrac{3x}{10} = \dfrac{1}{5}$

(vii) $\dfrac{x}{2} - \dfrac{1}{4} = \dfrac{x}{3} + \dfrac{1}{2}$

(viii) $\dfrac{2x - 3}{3x + 2} = \dfrac{-2}{3}$

(ix) $\dfrac{8p - 5}{7p + 1} = \dfrac{-2}{4}$

(x) $\dfrac{7y + 2}{5} = \dfrac{6y - 5}{11}$

(xi) $\dfrac{x + 5}{6} - \dfrac{x + 1}{9} = \dfrac{x + 3}{4}$

(xii) $\dfrac{3t + 1}{16} - \dfrac{2t - 3}{7} = \dfrac{t + 3}{8} + \dfrac{3t - 1}{14}$

III. Rijuana added a number repeatedly for 1000 times and added ome thousandth of 1,250 to obtain 1000th multiple of 55.25. Find the number.

IV: $x = 3 + 3 + 3$.........., $y = 5 + 5 + 5 + $.......... and $z = 7 + 7 + $...........; find the value of p when
$p = (x^2 + y^2 + z^2 + 2xy + 2yz + 2zx) - 3(x + y + z)$

Guided Practice C

1. Find the value of 'x' so that $l \parallel m$.

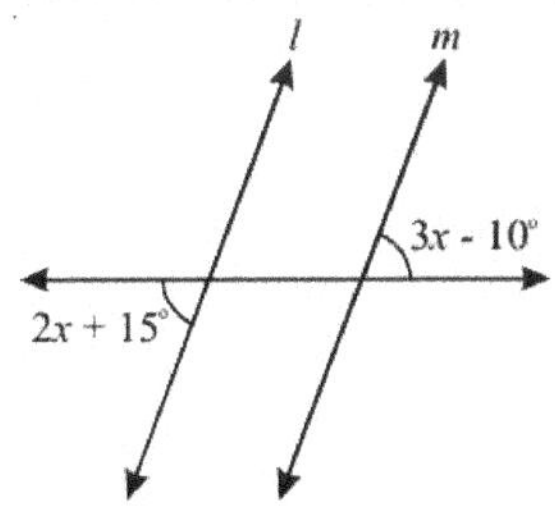

2. Quadrilaterals 1 and 8 are **kites**. Write down some properties of kites.

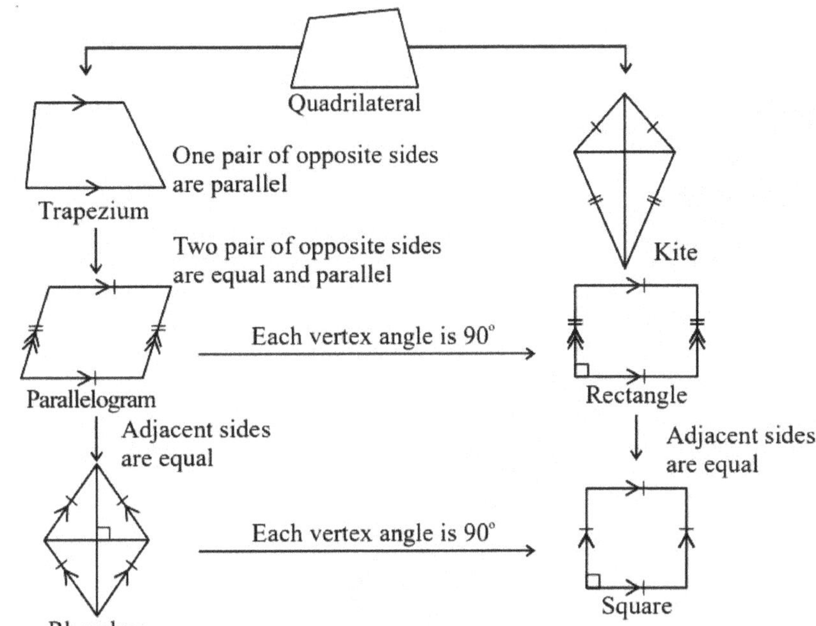

3. Simplify   (i) $2^2 \times \dfrac{3^2}{2^{-2}} \times 3^{-1}$ (ii) $(4^{-1} \times 3^{-1}) \div 6^{-1}$

4. Simplify and give reasons

(i) $(4^0 + 5^{-1}) \times 5^2 \times \dfrac{1}{3}$ (ii) $\left(\dfrac{1}{2}\right)^{-3} \times \left(\dfrac{1}{4}\right)^{-3} \times \left(\dfrac{1}{5}\right)^{-3}$

(iii) $(2^{-1} + 3^{-1} + 4^{-1}) \times \dfrac{3}{4}$ (iv) $\dfrac{3^{-2}}{3} \times (3^0 - 3^{-1})$

(v) $1 + 2^{-1} + 3^{-1} + 4^0$ (vi) $\left[\left(\dfrac{3}{2}\right)^{-2}\right]^2$

5: $x = \dfrac{4}{9}; y = \dfrac{43}{99}; z = \dfrac{124}{999}$; find the value of (x + y + z). Also find the value of $\left(\dfrac{x+y}{z}\right)^2$

6: Sonalika observed that a train can cross a light post in 45 seconds while running at a uniform speed of 76 km/h. This train can cross a platform of length 1 km 36 m in ….. m and ….seconds.

7: Neha subtracted 10 consecutive natural numbers repeatedly from a given number and obtained a result which is 55 less than the smallest five digit multiple of 5. Find the number.

8: Roshanlal formed a square sized shape by folding a circular wire of radius 44 cm. Find outer boundary and area of that shape.

Guided Practice D

1. How many different possible solutions can satisfy the following equation?

$$(x^2 - 5x + 5)^{(x^2 - 12x + 45)} = 1$$

2. A three digit number is such that the number N = 100a + 10b + c. Again the number is a product of two factors b and 10c + b. Find the number.

3. An integer is a palindrome when the same number is obtained when digits are reversed. 121,253, 132 etc. are all palindromes. Find a number n such that n^2 will be a palindrome with 6 digits.

4. Sum of the digits of a smallest possible number N is 18. Sum total of all the digits of 2N is 27. Find out the value of N.

5. What least number must be added to a six digit smallest number to make the number 1210214 divisible by 74.

6. Evaluate the following.

$$\left(\sqrt{2} + \sqrt{11} + \sqrt{13}\right)\left(\sqrt{2} + \sqrt{11} - \sqrt{13}\right)\left(\sqrt{2} - \sqrt{11} + \sqrt{13}\right)\left(-\sqrt{2} + \sqrt{11} - \sqrt{13}\right)$$

7. Each interior angles of a heptagon is obtuse. Angles are multiples of 9. Find the degrees of sums of the two largest angles.

8. A three digit number is multiplied by 3 and 1 added to it then the result is a reverse of the original number. Find the original number.

   [Hints: (100 a+ 10b + c)X3 +1 = 100c + 10b + a .

   100 a+ 10b + c = ?]

9. If ab $= a^b$ and $\dfrac{a}{b} = a^{3b}$, find b^{-a}

10. $0.33 < \dfrac{m}{n} < \dfrac{1}{3}$. Find the smallest possible value of n to satisfy the above mentioned relationship.

11. Find the smallest seven digit number which is divisible by 11. What are the two digits will be there in tens and ones place of that number?

12. Mark deposited $ 23,500 in his savings bank account which was offering 4% simple interest per year. Find the amount that Mark will obtain after a tenure of 4 years and 5 months.

13. -4.5 + 5.64 + _______ = 0. Make this equation true.

14. Solve the following

   a. $7 \times 20 - 2 \times 4 + 3^2 + 12 \div 4$

b. $\dfrac{\left(\sqrt[3]{0.125}+\sqrt[2]{.0064}\right)}{\sqrt[3]{1.331}-\sqrt[2]{0.0081}}$

c. If $x+\dfrac{1}{x}=9$ then find the value of $(2x-9)^2$

15. A shopkeeper purchased 16 dozen bananas at the rate of Rs 24 per dozen and found that 5% of his stock became non sellable. Rest of his stock was sold at the rate of Rs 30 per dozen. Find out the rate percent of his gain or loss incurred in this business.

16. Simplify the following: $7[120 - 2(4 + 3)^2 + 12] \div 2$

17. X = 0.3333... + 0.4444 + 0.9999.. Find the value of $\dfrac{x+1}{x-1} + \dfrac{x-1}{x+1}$

18. Shweta joined a Yoga Centre and her body weight was reduced from 76 kg to 65.6 kg. Find the percentage weight loss that she made during the tenure of her exercises.

19. Base of a triangle is reduced by 5% and its height is increased by 5%. Find the total percentage increase or decrease in the area of the triangle.

20. All the five sides of a regular pentagon is 12 cm each and apothem is 8 cm. find the area of this pentagon.

[Hints: The apothem of a regular polygon is a line segment from the center of the polygon perpendicular to a side.]

21. A ___________ angle is an angle with its vertex at the center of a circle whose sides are radii.

22. Calculate the total surface area of a cuboidal room of dimension 8mX6mX5m.

23. Arrange the following values in ascending and descending order:

24. What is the next number in the following sequence: 2, 4, 8, 16, ______, _______ ?

25. Write 3/7 and 5/9 in their corresponding decimal form. What are the common things in both the decimal form?

26. The cost of a camera is reduced by 10% to make it equivalent to another camera having a selling price calculated on the basis of 10% profit on the cost price of 21,850. Find the original cost price of the first camera.

27. 3% of 600 is _________ less than 5% of 500.

28. A college offers 25% of all seats of the Graduate programme to local candidates. Last year 125 local candidates got admission in that college. Find the total seat capacity available in that college for Graduate programmes.

29. A shopkeeper offers two discounts of value 5% and 8% on an item. Calculate the equivalent discount of two such consecutive discounts.

30. Population of a city increases at the rate of 10% of previous year's population. Calculate the population of a city in which population before two years was 125,000. Also calculate the population of that city after two year.

31. Parking lot of a school is represented by an expression:

$$\frac{3}{4}\left(2(2 + 4k) + 2\left(3 + \frac{5}{6} k\right)\right)$$

Convert this expression in simplest form.

32. 30% of a number is equal to 40% of another number. Calculate the ratio of both the number.

33. P = $\sqrt{20} - \sqrt{20} + \sqrt{20} - \sqrt{20} \dots \dots \dots \infty$. Find the value of $P^2 + 3P - 20$.

34. $\sqrt{15}$ = 3.88. Find the value of $\sqrt{\frac{5}{3}}$.

35. A person moved on towards countryside at 6 O'Clock. He travelled certain distance at an average speed of 4 km/h, and then another distance at 3 km/h and again a distance at an average speed of 6 km/h. After reaching he turned back and reached the place from where he had started. That time it was 12 noon in his wrist watch. Find the distance travelled by him.

[Ans: 24 km]

***.

Model Questions

1. 20% of 30% of 21,042 = ... X 1,002

2. A shopkeeper gained an amount equal to selling price of 2 breads by selling 20 breads. What is the gain percentage made by the shopkeeper?

3. Three bells toll at an interval of 20 s, 30 s and 40s respectively. Find the time interval after which all these three bells toll together.

4. A farmer can finish farm activities in 7 days while working 8 hours a day. Find in how many days he can finish farm activities while working 7 hours a day.

5. Rijuana observed that a train is taking 1.5 hours to reach another station. During return journey it took 1 h 20 m in covering up the same speed. Find average speed of that train.

6. Sum total of five consecutive multiples of 9 is equal to 135. Find product of third and fourth multiples if we arrange them all in ascending order.

7. $(1 + 2 + 3 + \ldots\ldots + 10{,}000) \times \left(\frac{1}{10{,}001} + \frac{1}{10001} + \cdots\ldots\ldots\ldots + 10{,}000 \; times\right)$ = ...

8. What fraction of all the shapes displayed below are polygons?

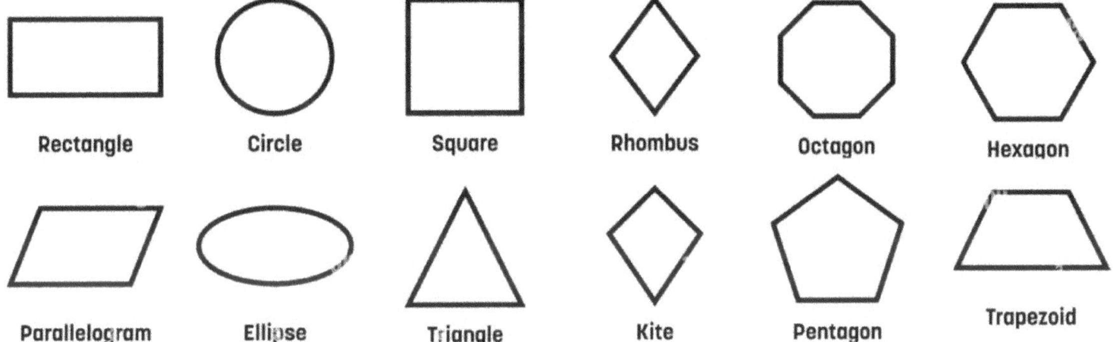

9. 30% of a = 50% of b = 70% of c; find the value of $\dfrac{a3 + b3 + c3}{abc}$ and $\dfrac{a^2 + b^2 + c^2}{ab+bc+ac}$

10. Two rectangles of dimension 3 cm X 4 cm and 6cm X 8 cm are arranged in such a way that their diagonals lie on the same line. Find total length of the line segment made up of two diagonals.

11. $\left(\sqrt{101} + \sqrt{101} + \cdots \; 10{,}000 \; times\right)\left(1 + \frac{1}{10{,}000}\right) X \sqrt{1 + \frac{1}{100}} \; X \; 10^{-5}$ =

    ....

12. $(x^2 + 4)(x^2 - 4)(x^4 - 16)$ = ...

13. $\left(\sqrt{36 + \sqrt{36 + \sqrt{36}\ldots\ldots\ldots\alpha}}\right)$ = ...

14. 5. x+ y = 2 and xy = 4; $(x^4 - y^4)(x^3 - y^3)$ = ...

15. Factorise: $(P^2 + q^2 - r^2 - 2pq)(P^2 + q^2 + r^2 + 2pq + 2qr + 2rs)$

16. $\left(\dfrac{\sqrt{3}+\sqrt{2}}{\sqrt{3}-\sqrt{2}}\right)\left(\dfrac{\sqrt{(5-2\sqrt{6})}}{\sqrt{5+2\sqrt{6}}}\right)\left(\dfrac{1}{1001}+\dfrac{1}{1001}+\cdots\ldots 1{,}000\ times\right) X \left(1-\dfrac{1}{2000}\right) X\ 1{,}999\ =\ \ldots\ldots\ldots$

17. $\left(\dfrac{1}{x}+\dfrac{1}{y}+\dfrac{1}{z}\right) = 55$, $(x + y + z) =\ 5$, $xy + yz + zx =$ ....

18. $(x\ \ -\ \ 1)(x^2\ \ +\ \ 1)(1\ \ +\ \ x)(x^4\ \ -\ \ 1)\ \ =\ \ 255;\ \ \ $ Find the value of $\dfrac{x^2+x+1}{x+1}\ X \left(\dfrac{1}{\sqrt{x}}+\dfrac{2}{\sqrt{x}}+\cdots\ldots+\dfrac{100}{\sqrt{x}}\right) X \sqrt[3]{6+x}$

19. $(pq + rs + st) = 256$; $p + q + r = 625$; $p^2 + r^2 + q^2 =$ ....

20. $\left(x +\dfrac{1}{x}\right) = 11\sqrt{11}$; $x^3 +\dfrac{1}{x^3} =$ .... ; $x^6 -\dfrac{1}{x^6} =$ .... ; $x^9 + x^4 - x^{-3} - x^{-9} =$ ....;

21. Factorization of the polynomial $(x - y)^2 a^2 + 2(x - y) (x + y) ab + b^2 (x + y)^2$ gives __________.

22. The polynomial $a^2 - b + ab - a$, on factorization, reduces to __________.

23. $\left(\sqrt{16 + \sqrt{16 + \sqrt{16 + \cdots\ldots\propto}}}\right)\left(\sqrt{81 + \sqrt{81 + \sqrt{81 + \cdots\ldots\propto}}}\right) =$ ....

24. $\left(x^3 +\dfrac{1}{x^3}\right) = 62$; $\sqrt{x^3} +\dfrac{1}{\sqrt{x^3}} =$ .... ; $\sqrt{x}^{-3} +\dfrac{1}{\sqrt{x}^{-3}} =$ ....

25. $\left(\dfrac{1}{356}+\dfrac{1}{356}+\dfrac{1}{356}+\cdots\ldots + 1{,}000\ times\right) X \left(1+\dfrac{1}{1000}\right) X\ 1{,}780\ =$ ....

26. 17. Simplify: $\left(\sqrt{30 + 2\sqrt{90} + 2\sqrt{110} + 2\sqrt{99}}\right) X \left(\sqrt{33 + 2\sqrt{120} + 2\sqrt{110} + 2\sqrt{132}}\right)$

27. $(1a^0 + 2a^1 + 3a^2 \ldots + 1000\ a^{999}) = 1001\ X\ 500$; Find the value of $(a^3 + 3 a^2 + 3a + 1)(a - 1)^3$

28. What least number should be added to six digit greatest number to make the value a perfect square number?

29. $(\sqrt{3} + \sqrt{3} + \sqrt{3} + \sqrt{3} + \cdots.\ 2{,}000\ times\,) X\ \dfrac{1}{\sqrt[3]{14+3\sqrt{3}+)}}\ X(1 -\dfrac{1}{\sqrt{3}}\,)\ \ \ =$ ....

30. Simplify the following:

a) $\sqrt{6 + \sqrt{6 + \sqrt{6 + \cdots\ldots\propto}}} + \sqrt{\dfrac{36}{81} + \sqrt{\dfrac{36}{81} + \sqrt{\dfrac{36}{81} + \cdots\ldots\propto}}} =$ ....

b) Product of three consecutive number a, b and c is equal to 3,000 . Find the value of $b^3 - b^2 +1$

c) Simplify: $\left(\dfrac{1}{\sqrt{109}} + \dfrac{1}{\sqrt{109}} + \dfrac{1}{\sqrt{109}}\ldots\ldots 13{,}000\ times\right) X \left(1+\dfrac{1}{13{,}000}\right) X \left(1+\dfrac{1}{108}\right) x\dfrac{1}{6{,}500} =$ ....

d) . $\left(1+\frac{1}{10}\right)\left(1+\frac{1}{11}\right)\ \ldots\ldots\ldots X\ \left(1+\frac{1}{10,000}\right) X\ \left(1-\frac{10,000}{10,001}\right) X\ 0.1021\ =$ ....

e) . $\frac{121}{169} X\ 1\frac{2}{11}\ X\frac{144}{196}\ X\ \left(1+\frac{1}{12}\right) X\ \left(1+\frac{2}{11}\right)\ =$ ....

31. Product of three consecutive numbers is equal to 210. Find the value of all the numbers.

32. Cistern A fills up an empty water tank in 45 minutes and cistern B fills up half of that water tank in half an hour. If both the cisterns kept open then the empty water tank will be filled up in ...... minutes.

33. Pundalik finishes a project work in 20 days while working 7 hours a day. The same work can be finished in .... days if Pundalik works for 5 hours a day.

34. Find square root of the following expression: $\left(33 + 2\sqrt{110} + 2\sqrt{132} + 2\sqrt{120}\ \right)$

35. $\dfrac{\sqrt[3]{1331} + \sqrt[2]{121} + 11}{1+\frac{1}{10}}\ X\ \dfrac{(1+2+3\ldots\ldots+10)}{1-\frac{1}{11}}\ \left(1+\frac{1}{2}\right)^{-1}\ =$ ....

36. Spontenian family reduced their monthly family expenditure to by curtailing their consumption of fuel by 25% so as to keep the budget on fuel intact. Find the percentage increase in the price of fuel.

37. Sum total of a number and its reciprocal is 8.125. Find sum total of the square and cube root of that number.

38. Railway fares of 1st, 2nd and 3rd classes between two stations were in the ratio 8 : 6 : 3. The fares of 1st and 2nd class were subsequently reduced by $\frac{1}{6}$ and $\frac{1}{12}$ respectively. If during a year, the ratio between the passengers of 1st, 2nd and 3rd classes was 9 : 12 : 26 and the total amount collected by the sale of tickets was Rs 1088, the collection from the passengers of 1st class was ______________.

39. Salary of Mark is increased by 16%. His previous salary was ____ % less than that of the increased salary.

40. Solve the following equation : $\frac{11}{144} X\ \frac{12}{169}\ X\ \frac{13}{121} X\ \frac{132}{341}\ X\ \frac{682}{1001}\ X\ \frac{13}{19}\ =$

41. What least number must added to the smallest six digit number and must be subtracted from the largest five digit number to make both of them a multiple of 11?

42. What least number must be added to 121.098 to make it a multiple of 1.001?

43. First tap can fill a water tank in 30 minutes and second tap can empty the half filled tank in 1.5 hours. By what time the empty tank will be filled up if both the tap kept open?

44. Half of a cake is given to all friends, half of the remaining portion of the cake retained by parents, one third of what remaining was distributed amongst John's classmates. Finally John received only 200 g of the cake. Find the quantity of that cake.

45. Sum total of a fraction and its reciprocal is equal to $2\frac{1}{6}$. Find the number.

46. 20% of 50% of a number is 2,050. Find the number.

47. 25: Simplify the following expressions

A: $\left(1 + \frac{1}{2}\right)\left(1 + \frac{1}{3}\right) \ldots \ldots \left(1 + \frac{1}{50,000}\right) X \left(1 - \frac{1}{50,001}\right) X\ 5\ X\ 10^4 = \cdots \ldots X\ 10^8$

B: $\frac{11}{12} X \frac{144}{121} X \frac{33}{49} x \frac{98}{12321} x \frac{1331}{2880} \left(1 - \frac{1}{3}\right)\left(1 - \frac{1}{33}\right)\left(1 - \frac{1}{49}\right) = \ldots\ldots\ldots\ldots\ldots$

C: $\frac{5}{11} x\ 121,121 + \frac{7}{15} x225,225 + \frac{11}{25} x\ 625,625\ = \ldots\ldots\ldots\ldots\ldots$

48. One seventh of three eleventh of a number exceeds 77,154 by 770,000. Find the number.

49. Cistern A can fill up a water tank in 45 minutes. Cistern B can fill up the same water tank in half of an hour. If both the cisterns are kept open then the water tank will be filled up completely in …… minutes.

50. Ms. Lonella bought   1/3 bushel of apples. She used 13/14 of the apples to make applesauce. What part of a bushel did she use for applesauce?

51. Piskilla observed that two bells toll together at an interval of 63 seconds. At what time intervals do these bells would toll individually? How many times do these bells toll in an interval of 10 minute 30 seconds?

52. Find out the smallest six digit common multiple of 2, 6, 8 and 11.

53. [(1.01 + 1.001 + 1.001 + 1.0001 + 1.00001) − 5.000001] − 0.9 = ………………

54. Sum total of five consecutive multiples of a natural number is equal to 25th multiple of 40. Find all the multiples of the given number.

55. Rijuana added 1.001 for 1,000 times to a given number to obtain four digit smallest multiple of 9. Find the number which was given.

56. (1.005 − 1.005 + 1.005 − 1.005 ………………… 10,008 times) − 5X1.005 = ……………

57. Somalia added seven digit greatest common multiple of 2,4 and 8 to smallest six digit multiple of 9 to obtain a natural number. 100 is multiplied to the result obtained by Somalia. Find out number of digits in that final result.

58. Cistern A, B and C can fill up a water tank individually in 1 hour, 1.5 hour and 2 hours respectively. If all the three cisterns kept open then find out the time taken by all the three cisterns jointly to fill up four such water tanks.

59. Mr. Bandarnayake boarded a domestic flight at 9:45 Hrs. The flight reached its final destiny in 1 H 34 minutes. New time zone shows local time increased by half of an hour. Find the time at the destiny which can be adjusted in the wrist watch of Mr. Bandarnayake.

60. What least number should be subtracted from five digit greatest nuber to obtain a common multiple of 11, 22 and 33?

Area and Perimeter

I: Find area of the following.

Figure		Measurements	Formula for area	Area of the given figure
	Square	Side of the square is 15 cm	$A = side \times side$	....
	Rectangle	Length = 20 cm Breadth = ...	$A = l \times b$	$280 cm^2$
	Triangle	Base = 5 cm Height = ...	$A = $	$60 cm^2$
	Parallelogram	Height = 7.6cm Base = ...	$A = b \times h$	$38 cm^2$
	Rhombus	$d_1 = 4$ cm $d_2 = 3$ cm	....	....

II: How many non-overlapping triangles can be accommodated in a polygon having seven sides?

III. One of the interior angle of a regular polygon is equal to 135^0. How many sides are there in that polygon?

IV: Area of a square is equal to 121 sq. cm. 16 such squares are arranged side by side to form a longest possible rectangle. Find lengh and breadth of that rectangle.

V: sum total of lengths of two parallel sides of a trapezium is equal to 12.12 cm. Distance between them is 5 cm. Find area of that trapezium.

VI: Trapezium…

Find the area of each trapezoid.

1. 21 yd / 4 yd / 12 yd

2. 9 ft / 12 ft / 12 ft

3. 9 cm / 11 cm / 17 cm

4. 1.6 in. / 1.1 in. / 3.4 in.

5. 14 mm / 16 mm / 21 mm

6. 14 / $9\frac{1}{2}$ ft / $11\frac{1}{2}$ ft / 8 ft

VII: Solve the following…

Kumar owns a plot near the main road as in the figure below. Unlike some other rectanglar plots in his neighbourhood, the plot has only a pair of parallel sides. So, it is nearly a trapezium in shape. Can you find out its area?

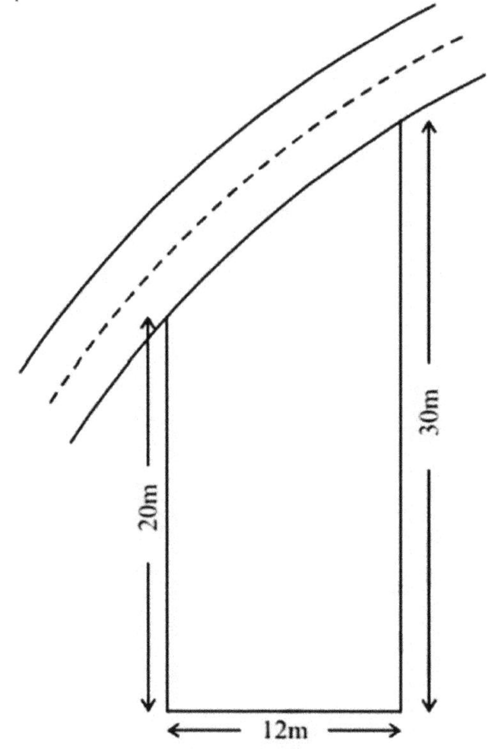

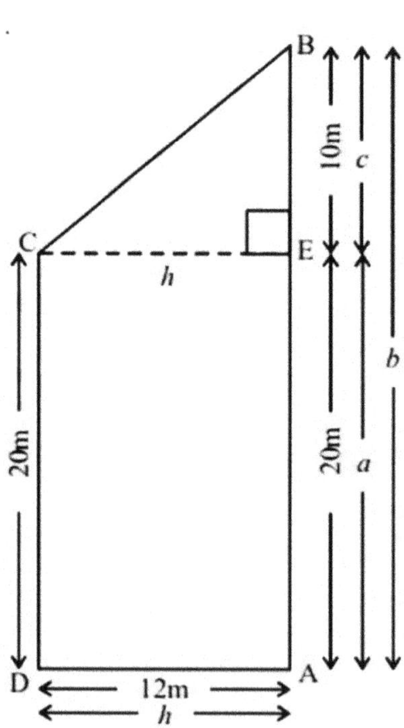

VIII: Estimation of Area…

Use formulas to find the areas. Estimate to help.

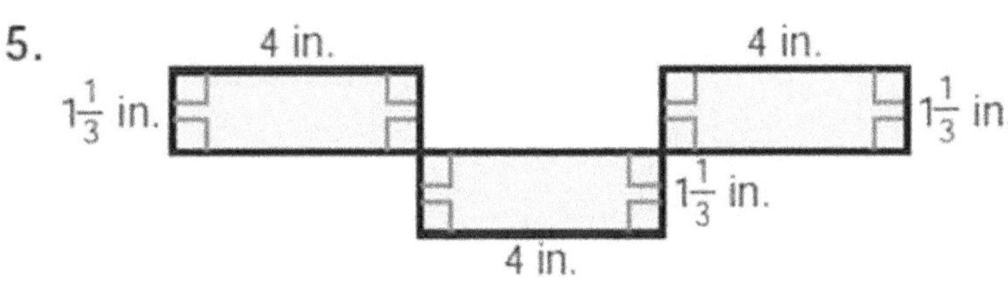

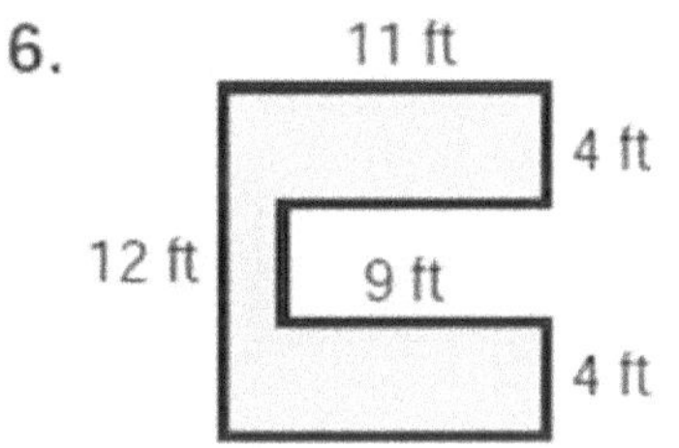

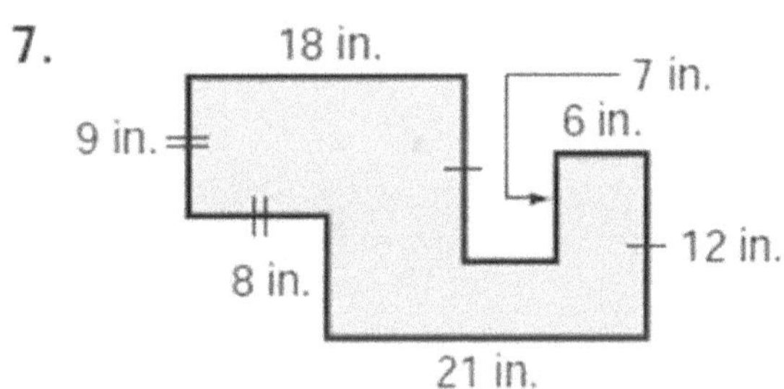

IX: Find area of the following:

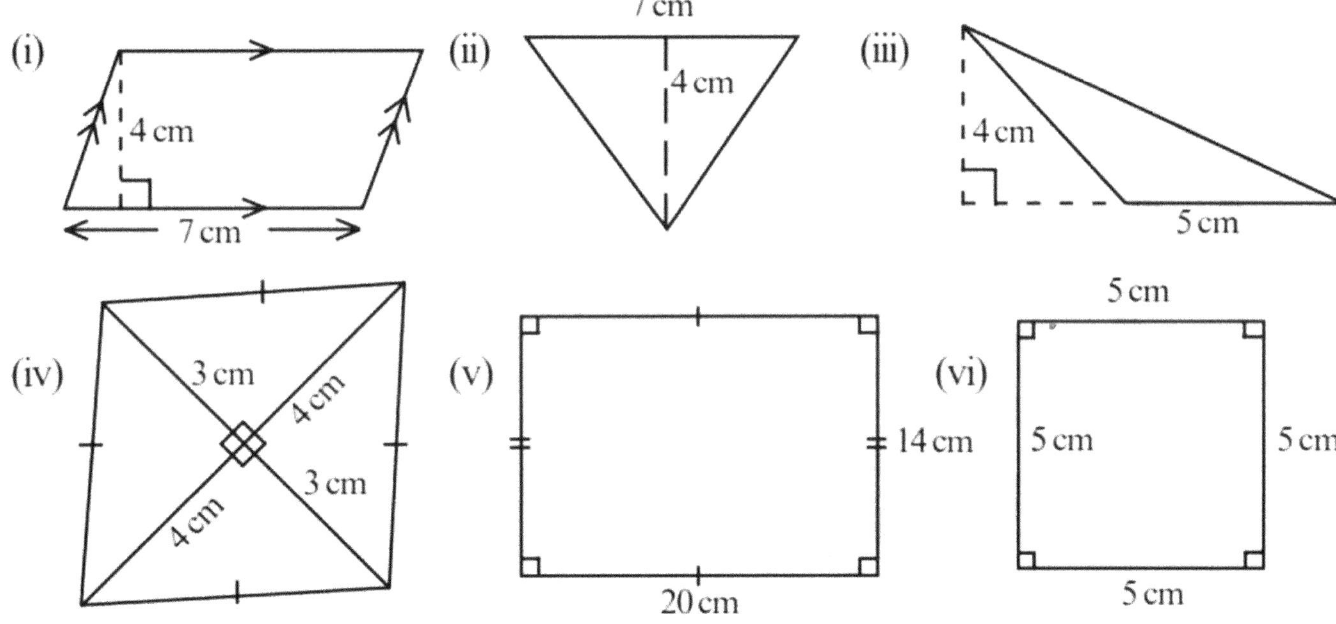

X: Pyramids…

Study these examples.

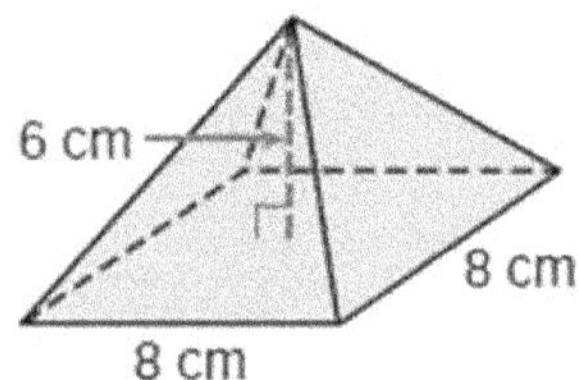

$V = \frac{1}{3} Bh$

$= \frac{1}{3} (8 \text{ cm})^2 \times 6 \text{ cm}$

$= 128 \text{ cm}^3$

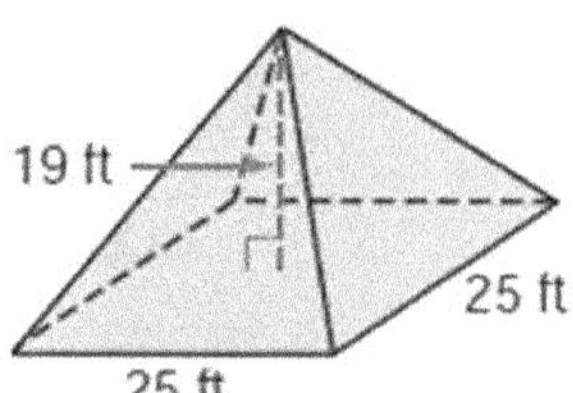

$V = \frac{1}{3} Bh$

$= \frac{1}{3} (25 \text{ ft})^2 \times 19 \text{ ft}$

$= 3958 \frac{1}{3} \text{ ft}^3$

Find the volume of each pyramid.

1.

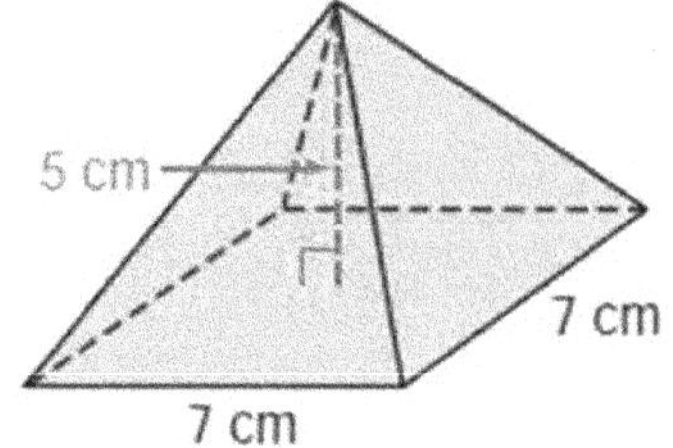

2.

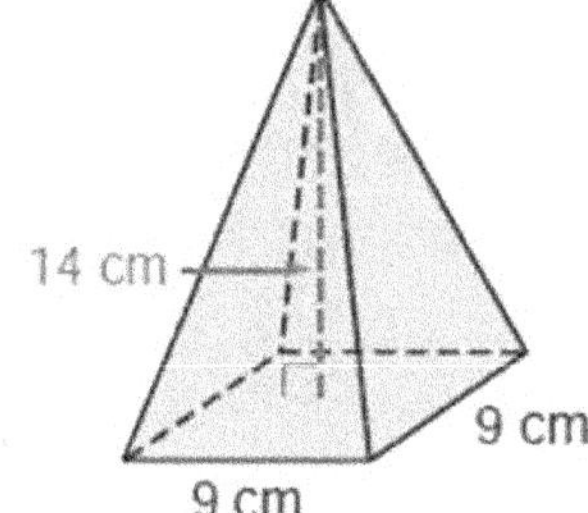

3.

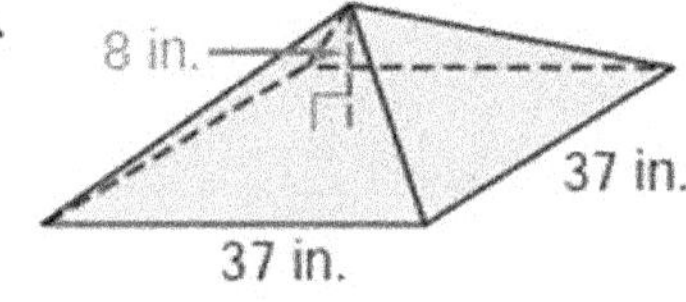

4.

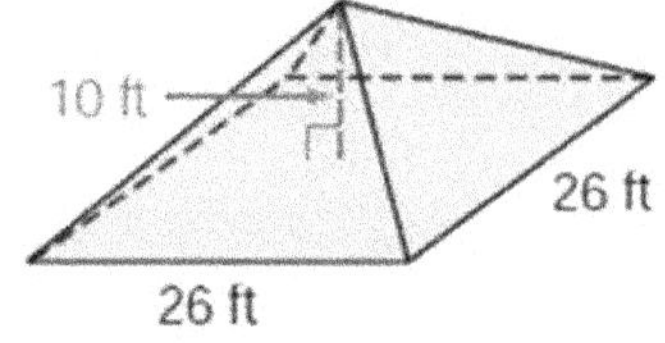

5.

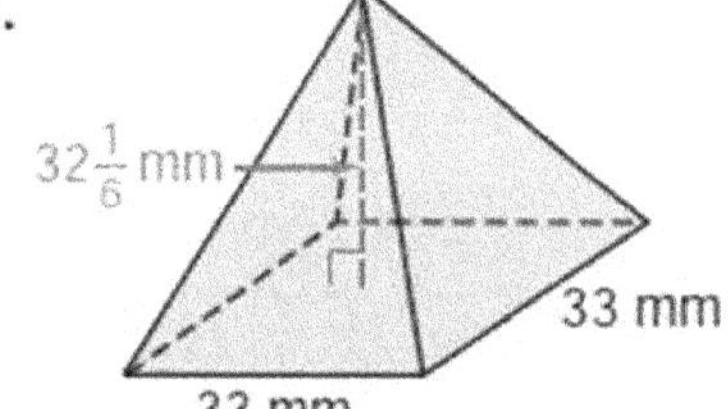

6.

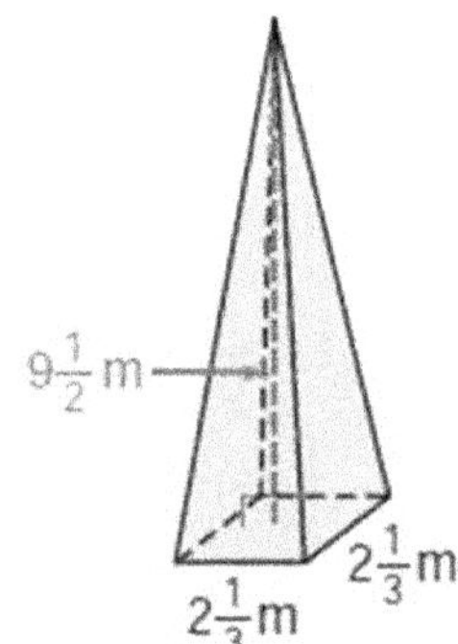

XI: Surface Area…

1.

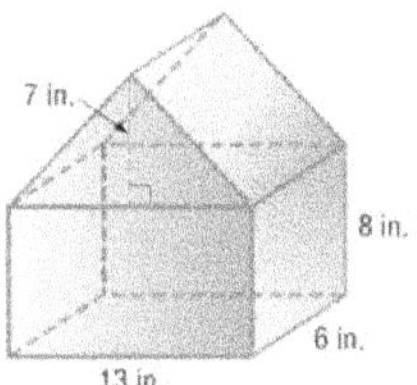

2.

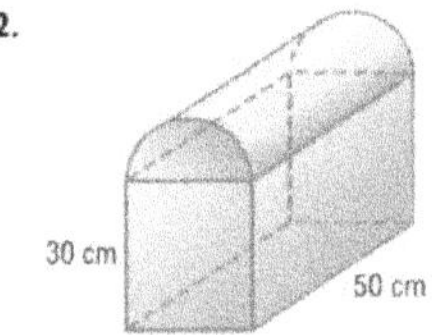

3.

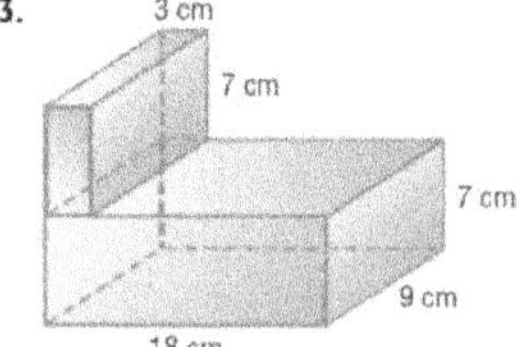

4.

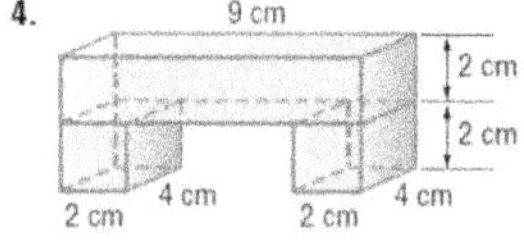

Revision Works

Unit 1

Write in Standard Form:

1. 39 hundreds + 39 thousands + 39 tens + 309 = ...
2. 309,000 + 3,090 + 309 + 30,900 = ...
3. 101,000,000 + 101,000 + 10,100 + 10,010 + 101 = ...
4. 109 thousands + 109 hundreds + 109 tens + 1009 = ...
5. 2011 + 20011 + 2000011 + 200000011 = ...

6. 4000 + 500 + 60 + 9   **7.** 20,000 + 2000 + 900 + 80 + 7

8. 400,000 + 300 + 50   **9.** 3,000,000 + 9000 + 40 + 8

10. 60,000,000 + 3,000,000 + 400,000 + 5000 + 7

11. 1,000,000,000 + 200,000,000 + 50,000,000 + 300 + 9

Write in expanded form.

12. 8998   **13.** 6745   **14.** 15,243   **15.** 37,418

16. 672,115   **17.** 350,001   **18.** 700,946   **19.** 2,200,002

20. 13,004,205   **21.** 604,003,020   **22.** 2,005,940,000

Choose the correct answer.

23. In the number 62,725, the 6 means:
    a. 6×1000 **b.** 6×100 **c.** $6 \times 100,000$ **d.** $6 \times 10,000$

24. In the number 2,784,349, the 2 means:
    a. 2×1000 **b.** $2 \times 10,000$ **c.** $2 \times 1,000,000$ **d.** $2 \times 100,000,000$

25. In the number 34,056,971,000, the 3 means:
    a. 3×1000 **b.** $3 \times 10,000$ **c.** $3 \times 10,000,000$ **d.** $3 \times 10,000,000,000$

26. (1.1 + 1.01 + 1.001 + 1.0001 + 1.00001 + 1.000001) − 6 = ...

27. 21 tens + 21 tenths + 201 tens + 201 thnths + 2,001 thousandths = ...

28. Two bells toll at an interval of 5 secoonds and 7 seconds respectively. How many times do these bells toll together in 1 m 10 seconds?

Unit 2

A **right angle** is an angle that has a measure of *exactly* 90°.

An **acute angle** is an angle that has a measure *less than* 90°.

An **obtuse angle** is an angle that has a measure *greater than* 90° but *less than* 180°.

A **straight angle** is an angle that has a measure of *exactly* 180°.

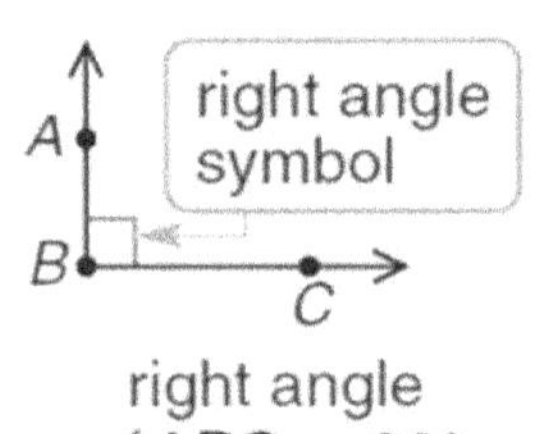

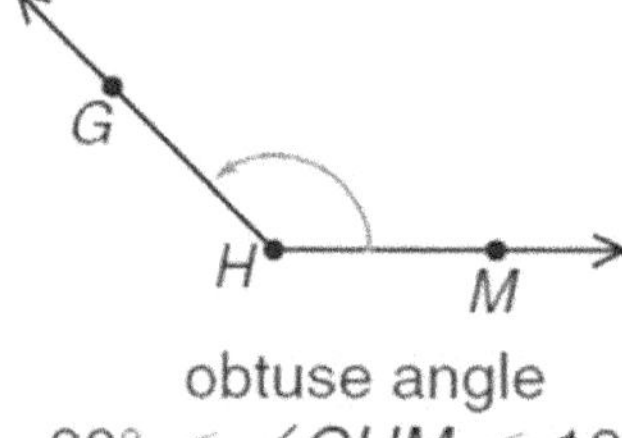

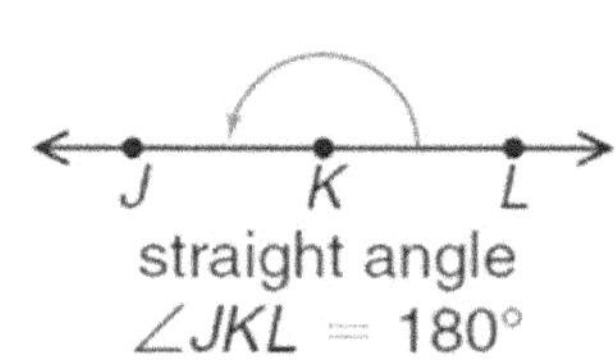

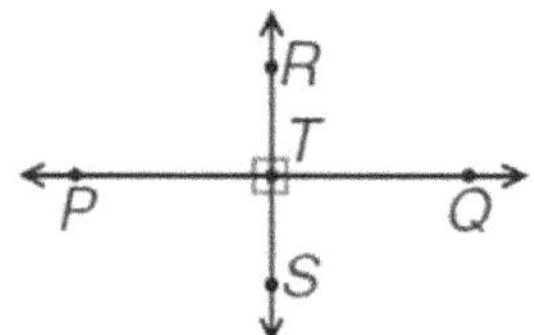

right angle	acute angle	obtuse angle	straight angle
∠ABC = 90°	∠DEF < 90°	90° < ∠GHM < 180°	∠JKL = 180°

Perpendicular lines are intersecting lines that form four right angles.

$\overleftrightarrow{RS}$ and $\overleftrightarrow{PQ}$ are perpendicular lines.
∠RTP, ∠PTS, ∠RTQ, and ∠QTS are right angles.

The symbol ⊥ means "is perpendicular to." $\overleftrightarrow{RS} \perp \overleftrightarrow{PQ}$

Write whether each angle is *acute, right, obtuse,* or *straight.*

1. 34°
2. 110°
3. 12°
4. 90°
5. 180°
6. 6°

7. 163°
8. 91°
9. 25°
10. 137°
11. 75°
12. 179°

13. 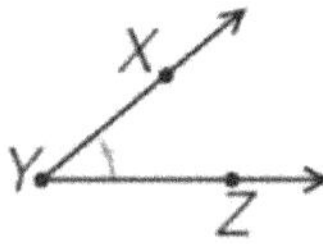

14. 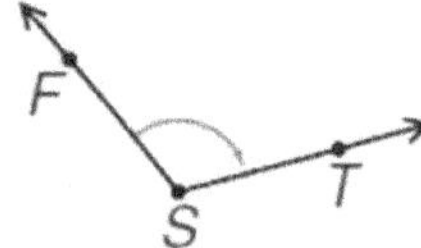

15. 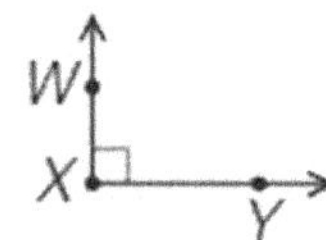

16. 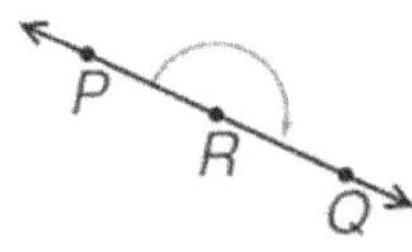

Name the following angles. Use the figure.

17. 4 acute angles

18. 2 right angles

19. a straight angle

20. 3 obtuse angles

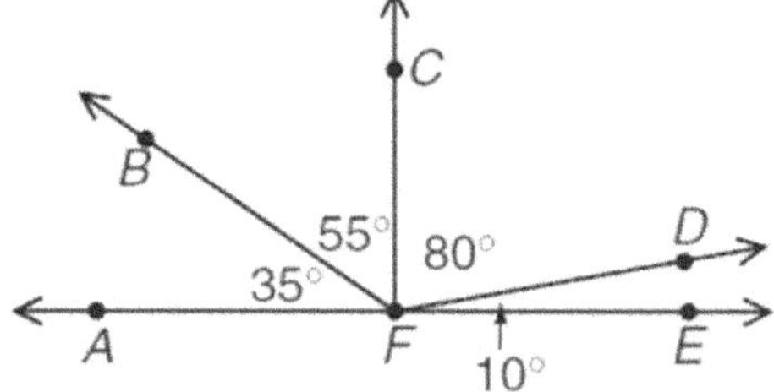

21. There are .... right angles in a regular quadrilateral.

22. Suplementary angle of a given angle is two times than its complementary angle. Find the angle.

***

Evaluation of Skills

Evaluation P

1. Use the Factor Theorem to determine whether g (x) is a factor of p (x) in each of the following cases

   (i) p (x)= $2x^3 + x^2 - 2x - 1$, g (x) = x + 1

   (ii) p(x)= $x^3 + 3x^2 + 3x + 1$, g (x) = x + 2

   (iii) p (x) = $x^3 - 4x^2 + x + 6$, g (x) = x − 3

2. What fraction of all the natural numbers starting from 1 to 20,000 are multiples of 125.

3. Observe the following number pttern and complete the sequence.

(1 + 3 + 5 + 7)	= 4 X 4	= ....;
(1 + 3 + ... + 19)	= 10 X 10	= ....;
(1 + 3 + ... + 99)	= ..... X ...	= ....;
(1 + 3 + ... + 999)	= .... X	= ....;
(1 + 3 + ... + 9,999)	= ... X	= ....;

4. For adding consecutive natural numbers we use a formula (an example is given)

   $(1 + 2 + 3 + ... + 10) = (10 + 1)X(10 \div 2)$; similarly for adding n consecutive numbers starting from 1 up to n in which n is an even number: $(1 + 2 + 3 + ... + n) = (n + 1)\left(\frac{n}{2}\right)$;

   Now calculate the following values:

   a) $(3 + 6 + 9 + ... + 3{,}000) = ...$

   b) $(5 + 10 + 15 + ... + 5{,}000) = ...$

   c) $(5 + 10 + 15 + ... + 5{,}000) X (2 + 4 + 6 + ... + 2{,}000) x (1001)^{-2} X (500)^5 = ...$

   d) $(6 + 12 + 18 + ... + 6{,}000) X (3 + 6 + 9 + ... + 3{,}000) x \left(1 + \frac{1}{1000}\right)^{-2} X (500)^{-3} X (18)^{--1} =$

   ....

   e) $(1 + 2 + 3 + ... + 50{,}000) X \left(1 + \frac{1}{50{,}000}\right)^{-2} X 2^3 X 50^3 X 10^{-8} X 5^{-3} = ... $;

   f) Sum total of 20 consecutive multiple of a number n = 1,890 ; find $(n^2 + 2n + 1)(n^2 - 2n + 1)$

   g) Sum total of 50 consecutive multiple of a number m exceeds 5th multiple of four digit smallest number by 100. Find the value of $(m^3 + 3m^2 + 3m + 1)(m^2 - 1)$

5. Sum total of 60 consecutive multiple of a number p is equal to 183,363. Find the smallest number.

Evaluation Q

1. What least number should be added to seven digit smallest number to make the value divisible by 11, 22 and 33 leaving remainder 8 in each case?
2. Find value of angles in each case…

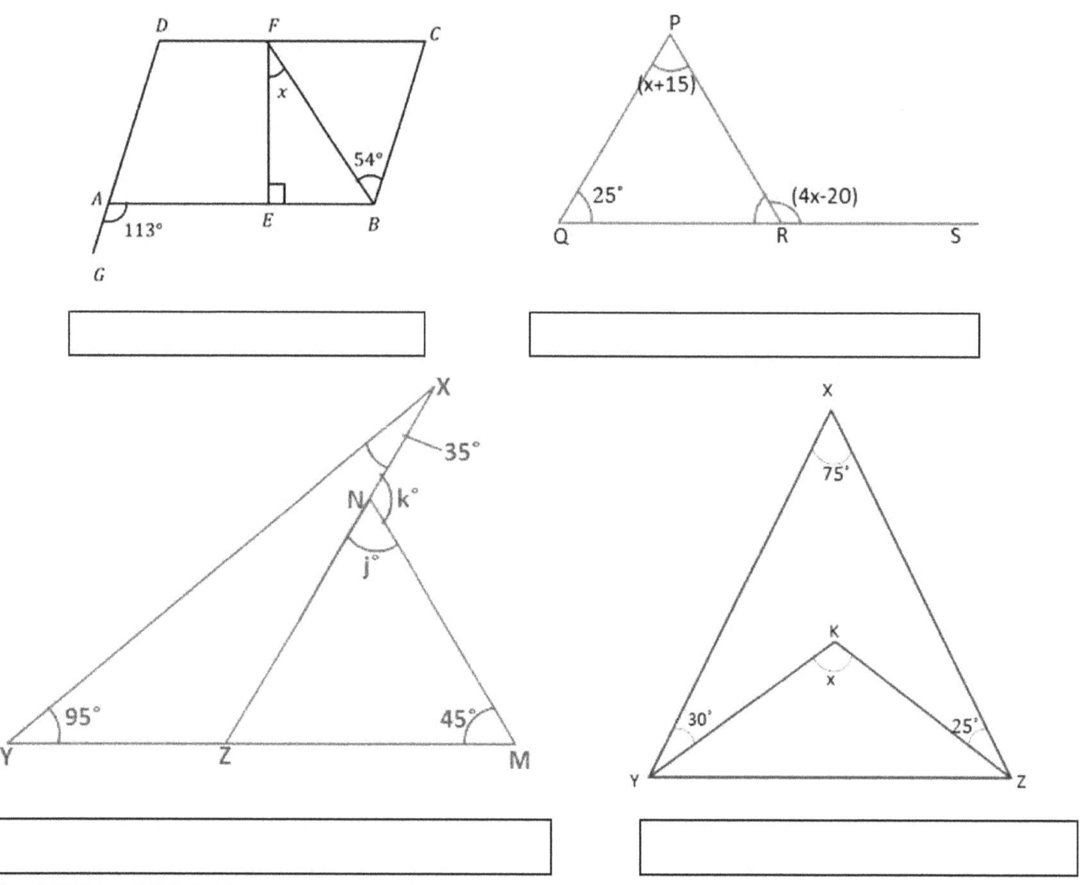

3. 20% of 30% of 21,042 = ... X 1,002
4. A shopkeeper gained an amount equal to selling price of 2 breads by selling 20 breads. What is the gain percentage made by the shopkeeper?
5. Three bells toll at an interval of 20 s, 30 s and 40s respectively. Find the time interval after which all these three bells toll together.
6. A farmer can finish farm activities in 7 days while working 8 hours a day. Find in how many days he can finish farm activities while working 7 hours a day.
7. Rijuana observed that a train is taking 1.5 hours to reach another station. During return journey it took 1 h 20 m in covering up the same speed. Find average speed of that train.
8. Sum total of five consecutive multiples of 9 is equal to 135. Find product of third and fourth multiples if we arrange them all in ascending order.
9. $(1 + 2 + 3 + \ldots + 10{,}000) \times \left(\dfrac{1}{10{,}001} + \dfrac{1}{10001} + \cdots \ldots \ldots \ldots + 10{,}000\ times\right)$ = ………

II. Solve the following…..

Add or subtract. Write in simplest form.

1. $\frac{3}{4} + \left(-\frac{1}{6}\right)$

2. $-\frac{5}{8} + \frac{1}{2}$

3. $-\frac{4}{9} + \left(-\frac{2}{3}\right)$

4. $\frac{7}{8} - \frac{3}{4}$

5. $\frac{7}{13} - \frac{2}{9}$

6. $\frac{14}{15} - \left(-\frac{12}{21}\right)$

7. $-3\frac{2}{5} + 1\frac{5}{6}$

8. $3\frac{5}{8} - 1\frac{1}{3}$

9. $-4\frac{7}{12} - \left(-3\frac{7}{72}\right)$

10. $\left(1 - \frac{1}{2}\right)\left(1 - \frac{1}{3}\right) \dots \dots \left(1 - \frac{1}{1000}\right) \ X \ 101,101 \ X \frac{1}{101} \ = $ …………………………

Add or subtract. Write in simplest form.

11. $\frac{1}{4} + \left(-\frac{7}{12}\right)$

12. $-\frac{3}{8} + \frac{5}{6}$

13. $-\frac{6}{7} + \left(-\frac{1}{2}\right)$

14. $-\frac{5}{9} + \left(-\frac{3}{8}\right)$

15. $\frac{1}{3} - \frac{7}{8}$

16. $\frac{4}{5} - \left(-\frac{2}{15}\right)$

17. $-\frac{2}{9} - \left(-\frac{3}{11}\right)$

18. $-\frac{7}{15} - \left(-\frac{12}{25}\right)$

19. $3\frac{1}{5} + \left(-8\frac{1}{2}\right)$

20. $1\frac{1}{6} + \left(-6\frac{2}{3}\right)$

21. $8\frac{3}{7} - \left(-6\frac{1}{2}\right)$

22. $7\frac{3}{4} - \left(-1\frac{1}{8}\right)$

23. $-4\frac{3}{4} - 5\frac{5}{8}$

24. $-8\frac{1}{3} - 4\frac{5}{6}$

25. $-15\frac{5}{8} + 11\frac{2}{3}$

26. $-22\frac{2}{5} + 15\frac{5}{6}$

III. Solve the following:

1. There were 34.8 crore internet users in the world during 2022. There will be 125% increase in the number of users during forthcoming years. What would be the estimated number of users during forthcoming year?

2. A shopkeeper purchased 300 bulbs at the rate of Rs 40 each. Hoever 15 bulns were fused. Rest of the bulbs were sold at the rate of Rs 50 each. Find his loss or gain percentage.

3. Price marked on an electronics item was Rs 21,034/-. There was 20% discount on that item. Find the amount payable by any customer.

4. 15% of 20% of a number exceeds sixth multiple of seven digit smallest odd number by 480.. Find fifth multiple of that number.

5. What percentage of a seven digit smallest multiple of 9 become 250,002?

6. Sum total of predecessor and successor of six digit greatest number has ………. Digits in all.

7. (1 + 2 + 3 + ….. +100) – (1 + 2 + …..+10) = ……………..

Evaluation R

3. $(x^2 + 4)(x^2 - 4)(x^4 - 16) = $ ....

....

4. $\left(\sqrt{36 + \sqrt{36 + \sqrt{36}\ldots\ldots\infty}}\right)$ =

5. $x + y = 2$ and $xy = 4$; $(x^4 - y^4)(x^3 - y^3) = $ .....

6. Factorise: $P^2 + q^2 - r^2 - 2pq$

7. $\left(\dfrac{\sqrt{3} + \sqrt{2}}{\sqrt{3} - \sqrt{2}}\right)\left(\dfrac{\sqrt{(5 - 2\sqrt{6})}}{\sqrt{5 + 2\sqrt{6}}}\right)\left(\dfrac{1}{1001} + \dfrac{1}{1001} + \cdots \ldots 1,000 \ times\right) X \left(1 - \dfrac{1}{2000}\right) X\ 1,999\ = $ ....

8. $\left(\dfrac{1}{x} + \dfrac{1}{y} + \dfrac{1}{z}\right) = 55$, $(x + y + z) = 5$, $xy + yz + zx = $ ....

9. $(x - 1)(x^2 + 1)(1 + x)(x^4 - 1) = 255$; Find the value of $\dfrac{x^2 + x + 1}{x + 1}$ $X \left(\dfrac{1}{\sqrt{x}} + \dfrac{2}{\sqrt{x}} + \cdots \ldots + \dfrac{100}{\sqrt{x}}\right) X \sqrt[3]{6 + x}$

10. $(pq + rs + st) = 256$; $p + q + r = 625$; $p^2 + r^2 + q^2 = $ ....

11. $\left(x + \dfrac{1}{x}\right) = 11\sqrt{11}$; $x^3 + \dfrac{1}{x^3} = $ .... ; $x^6 - \dfrac{1}{x^6} = $ .... ; $x^9 + x^4 - x^{-3} - x^{-9} = $ ....;

12. Factorization of the polynomial $(x - y)^2 a^2 + 2(x - y)(x + y) ab + b^2 (x + y)^2$ gives __________.

13. The polynomial $a^2 - b + ab - a$, on factorization, reduces to __________.

14. $\left(\sqrt{16 + \sqrt{16 + \sqrt{16 + \cdots \ldots \infty}}}\right)\left(\sqrt{81 + \sqrt{81 + \sqrt{81 + \cdots \ldots \infty}}}\right) = $ ....

15. $\left(x^3 + \dfrac{1}{x^3}\right) = 62$; $\sqrt{x^3} + \dfrac{1}{\sqrt{x^3}} = $ .... ; $\sqrt{x}^{-3} + \dfrac{1}{\sqrt{x}^{-3}} = $ ....

16. $\left(\dfrac{1}{356} + \dfrac{1}{356} + \dfrac{1}{356} + \cdots \ldots + 1,000 \ times\right) X \left(1 + \dfrac{1}{1000}\right) X\ 1,780\ = $ ....

17. Simplify: $\left(\sqrt{30 + 2\sqrt{90} + 2\sqrt{110} + 2\sqrt{99}}\right) X \left(\sqrt{33 + 2\sqrt{120} + 2\sqrt{110} + 2\sqrt{132}}\right)$

18. $(1a^0 + 2a^1 + 3a^2 \ldots\ldots + 1000\ a^{999}) = 1001\ X\ 500$; Find the value of $(a^3 + 3a^2 + 3a + 1)(a - 1)^3$

19. What least number should be added to six digit greatest number to make the value a perfect square number?

20. $(\sqrt{3} + \sqrt{3} + \sqrt{3} + \sqrt{3} + \cdots . 2,000 \ times) X \ \dfrac{1}{\sqrt[3]{14 + 3\sqrt{3}+)}} \ X (1 - \dfrac{1}{\sqrt{3}}) \ = $ ....

21. 30% of a = 50% of b = 70% of c; find the value of $\dfrac{a3 + b3 + c3}{abc}$ and $\dfrac{a^2 + b^2 + c^2}{ab + bc + ac}$

Rounding and Estimation

We use rounding and estimation to check exact answers which is obtained after performing any mathematical operation.

Consider following examples.

$8,309,000 - 777,625 = \underline{\ ?\ }$

$$\begin{array}{r} 8,309,000 \\ -\ \ 777,625 \\ \hline 7,531,375 \end{array}$$

Add to check:
$7,531,375 + 777,625 = 8,309,000$

$3 - 0.7185 = \underline{\ ?\ }$

$$\begin{array}{r} 3.0000 \\ -\ 0.7185 \\ \hline 2.2815 \end{array}$$

$3 = 3.0000$

Add to check:
$2.2815 + 0.7185 = 3.0$

Both the answers are reasonable.

Compute mentally.

1. $1286 - 1000$

2. $0.98 - 0.08 - 0.8$

3. $0.98 - 0.9 - 0.07$

4. $14,500 - 1500$

5. $7 - 0.5\ 25.$

6. $75 - 4.25 - 1.01$

7. $0.525 - 0.5$

8. $262,000 - 42,000$

9. $242 - 0.75 - 0.2$

Aid Box:

Estimate by rounding. Then find the difference.

1.
$$\begin{array}{r} 0.586 \\ -\ 0.492 \\ \hline \end{array}$$

2.
$$\begin{array}{r} 2.3004 \\ -\ 0.1544 \\ \hline \end{array}$$

3.
$$\begin{array}{r} \$856,079 \\ -\ 622,003 \\ \hline \end{array}$$

4.
$$\begin{array}{r} 5,034,012 \\ -\ 316,948 \\ \hline \end{array}$$

5.
$$\begin{array}{r} 23,594,550 \\ -\ 7,008,142 \\ \hline \end{array}$$

6.
$$\begin{array}{r} 12.80765 \\ -\ 9.6153 \\ \hline \end{array}$$

7.
$$\begin{array}{r} 596,081,009 \\ -\ 574,116,025 \\ \hline \end{array}$$

8.
$$\begin{array}{r} 403.0078 \\ -\ 86.25 \\ \hline \end{array}$$

Align and estimate by rounding. Then find the difference.

9. $0.91 - 0.745$

10. $0.9158 - 0.7444$

11. $8 - 2.04735$

12. $7,106,009 - 248,310$

13. $20,700.675 - 700.775$

14. $1 - 0.3856$

15. $\$1,012,481.37 - 926,399.76$

16. $5,391,602,140 - 4,387,899,000$

Aid Box 2: …

Estimate using rounding. Then find the sum.

1.   7
  + 8.56

2.   6.4922
  + 15.58

3. $11,873.52
  +   4,906.09

4.   2,527,004,609
  +   38,211,073

5.   3,465,892
  + 2,396,087

6.   1.6902333
  + 0.7197807

7.   526,381,485
  + 574,626,009

8.   3,245,840,900
  +   80,059,275

9. 3.905 + 4.96

10. 0.4791 + 1.085

11. 0.10907 + 0.092

12. 0.2613 + 0.45 + 0.852

13. 0.5441 + 9.3 + 0.4637

14. 567,074 + 96,132 + 8650

15. 9,732,785 + 13,820,465

Aid Box 3:..

Estimate the sum or difference. Use front-end estimation with adjustments.

1.   31.6
  + 18.1

2.   68.7
  − 63.9

3.   7.5
  − 2.9

4.   9.1
  − 3.6

5.   0.87
  − 0.54

6.   0.74
  − 0.15

7.   76.67
  23.89
  + 69.47

8.   16.34
  44.59
  + 39.07

9.   0.66
  0.7
  + 0.19

10.   0.84
  0.59
  + 0.8

Estimate the sum or difference by rounding.

11.   18.1534
  + 7.0901

12.   4.8359
  − 0.7473

13.   0.45601
  + 0.06428

14.   4371.5902
  − 127.3246

15.   386,002,444
  − 49,624,973

16.   2.361912
  − 0.19008

17.   952.0667
  232.608
  + 351.03991

18.   7.30267
  45.37
  + 0.84652

19. During a tour of Europe, Alfredo flew 112.5 km, 41.8 km, and 109.5 km. Estimate the total distance that Alfredo travelled.

20. Weekly sales report of a shopkeeper in INR is recorded in the system box as 123.65, 1021.32, 1098.65, 1231.54, 1043.54 and 20200.43 respectively for six consecutive days. Sunday was leave day. Estimate total sales report of that week in INR.

21. Smallest possible six digit odd number which is divisible by 2, 3, 5 and 9 is …………………

Revision Works

Write each number in standard form.

1. three ten thousandths

2. nine trillion, four hundred thousand, twenty

3. sixty-seven and sixty-eight millionths

Write each number in expanded form using exponents.

4. four and eighty-three thousandths

5. 200,070,040,333

6. 734

7. 329,050

8. 24,082,006

Write in order from greatest to least.

9. 0.3014; 3.014; 0.0314; 0.314

10. 0.031289; 3.001289; 33.1289

Round each number to its underlined place.

11. 6,<u>7</u>45,199

12. 39<u>9</u>.97022

13. 11,542,3<u>9</u>1.956

14. 12,094.<u>7</u>85

15. 1020<u>2</u>.93

16. 209.<u>9</u>80

Write each as an algebraic expression. Use n as your variable.

17. 8 more than a number

18. a number decreased by 200

Write in standard form:

19: 21 tens + 21 hundreds + 21 thousands

20: 101 hundreds + 101 thousandths

21: 91 thousands + 121 hundredths

22: 61 tens + 109 hundreds + 111 hundredths

23. Rijuana needs _________ saplings for planting by the side of a 10 km road on both the sides at an interval of 20 m.

24. Total cost of 4 cakes and 6 snacks is Rs 98. In another combination total cost of 7 cakes and 5 snacks is Rs 110. Find total cost of 3 cakes and 17 snacks.

25: Three bells toll at an interval of 4 seconds, 6 seconds and 8 seconds respectively. How many times do they toll together in 10 minutes?

26: Rishabh prepared five digit smallest and five digit greatest numbers without repeating any of the digits twice. Find the sum total of both the numbers.

27: What fraction of all the natural numbers from 11 to 34 are prime numbers?

28: _________ is the least number of six digits divisible by 9.

29: What fraction of the following figure is shaded?

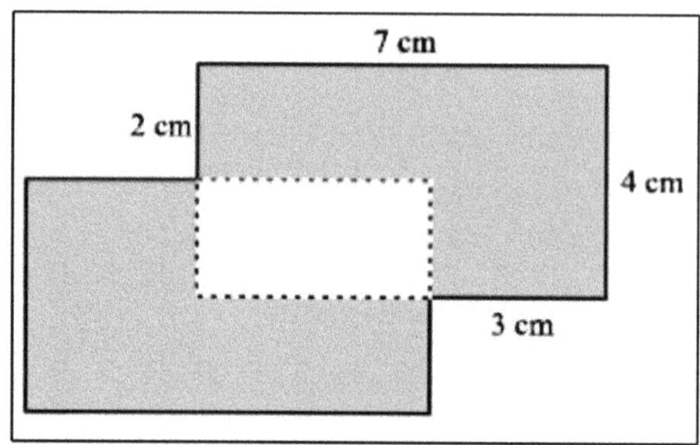

30. 10% of 10% of a number is 4. Find the number.

31. Equivalent fraction of 3.5% = __________.

32: 20% of 60% of a number exceeds six digit smallest multiple of 12 by 96. Find fifth multiple of that number.

Aid Box …

Write each number in expanded form two ways.

1. 46,000,000

2. eight thousand, eighty and eighty-three millionths

Write each number in standard form.

3. 10^5

4. $(2 \times 10^3) + (5 \times 10^2) + (4 \times 10^0) + (9 \times 10^{-2})$

Write in order from least to greatest.

5. 0.7968; 0.7000; 0.7909

6. 1.058; 1.0058; 10.0058

Round each number to its greatest place.

7. 3,429,099

8. 0.96153301

9. 954,313.8701

**Estimate using front-end estimation with adjustments.
Then find the sum or difference.**

10. 1229.13 + 756 + 3890.88

11. 1,007,291 − 2,364.065

12: 1.01 + 1.001 + 1.0001 + 1.00001 + 0.000001 − 4.001 = ...

Simple Multiplication

Repeated addition is similar to multiplication.

(5 + 5 + ... 1,000 times) = 5 X 1,000   = 5,000

In another number pattern we have ..

(1 + 3 + 5)	= 3 X 3	= 9;
(1 + 3 + 5 + 7)	= 4 X 4	= 16;
(1 + 3 + 5 + 7 + 9 + 11)	= 6 X 6	= 36;
(1 + 3 + 5 .... + 49)	= 25 X 25	= 625;

Similarly sum of 100 consecutive odd numbers   = 100 X 100   = 10,000;

Aid Box 1:

Estimate the product.

5. $\begin{array}{r} 335 \\ \times 129 \\ \hline \end{array}$ 6. $\begin{array}{r} 824 \\ \times 617 \\ \hline \end{array}$ 7. $\begin{array}{r} 925 \\ \times 376 \\ \hline \end{array}$ 8. $\begin{array}{r} 5847 \\ \times 219 \\ \hline \end{array}$ 9. $\begin{array}{r} 7932 \\ \times 324 \\ \hline \end{array}$

10. $\begin{array}{r} \$44.25 \\ \times 142 \\ \hline \end{array}$ 11. $\begin{array}{r} \$53.38 \\ \times 319 \\ \hline \end{array}$ 12. $\begin{array}{r} \$847.69 \\ \times 293 \\ \hline \end{array}$ 13. $\begin{array}{r} \$795.20 \\ \times 498 \\ \hline \end{array}$

14. 10.6×23 15. 5.52×1.78 16. 0.9×13.6 17. 137×2.85

18. 6235×3.7 19. 2.8×31.89 20. 3.2×14.79 21. 0.7×103.95

22. $10.7 \times 2.9 \times 28.04$ 23. $1.5 \times 2.8 \times 12.1$ 24. $4.3 \times 18.07 \times 1.79$

25. $3.54 \times 13.9 \times 428$ 26. $19.45 \times 24 \times 2.3$ 27. $7.81 \times 67.19 \times 112$

28. Product of two consecutive numbers is equal to 999,000. Find the numbers.

29. $\left(1 + \frac{1}{2}\right)\left(1 + \frac{1}{3}\right)\left(1 + \frac{1}{4}\right) \ldots \ldots \left(1 + \frac{1}{10,000}\right) X \left(1 - \frac{1}{10,001}\right) = \ldots \ldots \ldots \ldots$

30. Two numbers, each rounded to the nearest ten, have a product of 800. What are two possible numbers?

Aid Box 2…

Write the decimal point in each product.

1. $\quad$ 5.9 $\times\quad$ 3 —— 1 7 7	**2.** 0.2 3 5 $\times\qquad$ 7 ———— 1 6 4 5	**3.** $\quad$ 9.2 7 $\times\qquad$ 1.5 ———— 1 3 9 0 5	**4.** $\qquad$ 0.4 6 3 $\times\qquad$ 0.2 2 6 ———— 0 1 0 4 6 3 8	**5.** 1 2.9 2 $\times\qquad$ 0.7 ———— 9 0 4 4

Multiply. Round to the nearest cent when necessary.

6. $\quad$ 0.9 $\times$ 22	**7.** $\quad$ 0.7 $\times$ 79	**8.** $\quad$ 0.59 $\times\quad$ 43	**9.** $\quad$ 0.47 $\times\quad$ 21	**10.** $\quad$ 0.32 $\times\quad$ 73
11. $\quad$ 0.43 $\times$ 0.19	**12.** $\quad$ 0.61 $\times$ 0.93	**13.** $\quad$ 0.163 $\times\quad$ 0.03	**14.** $\quad$ 0.911 $\times\quad$ 9.11	**15.** $\quad$ 0.414 $\times$ 0.72
16. $\quad$ 13.5 $\times\quad$ 9.2	**17.** $\quad$ 0.20 $\times\quad$ 9.1	**18.** $8.05 $\times\quad$ 1.9	**19.** $9.20 $\times\quad$ 4.5	**20.** $10.50 $\times\qquad$ 8

21. $59.50 $\times$ 2.4 $\qquad$ **22.** 8.5 $\times$ 0.6 $\qquad$ **23.** 4.12 $\times$ 1.8 $\qquad$ **24.** 8.74 $\times$ 3.15

25. 9 $\times$ $56.95 $\qquad$ **26.** 1.5 $\times$ 8.00 $\qquad$ **27.** 6.2 $\times$ 9.5 $\qquad$ **28.** 4.75 $\times$ $85

29. Complete the number pattern:

11 X 11 $\qquad$ = 121;

111 X _____ $\qquad$ = 12321;

_____ X ________ $\qquad$ =1234321;

30. There are two combinations of packs containing pens and pencils. Packet one containing 6 pens and 5 pencils costs Rs 128. Packet B containing 5 pens and 6 pencils costs Rs 103. Calculate the cost of a new pack containing 10 pens and 10 pencils of such type?

31. Product of three consecutive multiple of 100 is equal to sixth multiple of 10^5. Find sum total of all these three multiples of 100.

32. In a test that Smitha wrote, the ratio of the right answers to the wrong answers that she got was 13:8. If she got 32 answers wrong, then she got ______ answers right.

33. In a kitty bank, number of 25 paisa coins is 23 times the number of 50 paisa coins. If there are 336 coins in the kitty bank, find the total amount of money in the collection.

.

Problem Solving Abilities

1. There were 6416 trees in a forest. In another forest there are three eighth more trees than the first one. Trees in third forest are equal to 550 less than those of all the trees of both the first and second forest put together. Arrange these forests in accord to the increasing number of trees.

2. Find the perimeter of a figure formed by joining three equilateral triangles of side 23.23 cm each.

3. Nithin is 40 m South West of Kavita. Mohini is 430 m South East of Kavita. Mohini is in which direction of Nithin ?

4. Add: $16\frac{9}{10} + 106\frac{19}{100} + 21\frac{3}{1000} =$

5. Veena rides her bike to the park for 18 minutes at an average speed of 9 m per second to meet a friend. Veena arrives at the park at 11:00 a.m. and stays there for 58 minutes. Her friend will arrive there at 12:15 p.m. they had a meeting for 32 minutes.
   Try to answer the following questions.
   A. What is the distance between the park and Veena's house?
   B. How long could Veena have to wait for her friend?
   C. How long does Veena stay at the park?
   D. When will Veena leave to go home?

6. Complete the number pattern:
   a. 9, 12, 15, 18, 21, 24, 27, ___, ___, ___
   b. 1, 1,2 , 3, ___, 8 , 13, ______ , ____
   c. 144, 121, 100, _____, _____ , 49, 36, 25, ____ , ____, 4, 1.
   d. $\frac{11}{100}, \frac{12}{110}, \frac{13}{120},$ ________, ________, ________ .

7. $1 + 2 + 3 + \ldots + 100 \quad = (100 + 1)X\frac{100}{2} \quad = 101\,X\,50 = 5{,}050$

Find the value of $1 + 2 + 3 + \ldots + 1{,}000$

8 . Which shape could be one of the faces of a cylinder?

9 . Arrange the following shapes as per their increasing number of faces.
Cylinder, Sphere, Cuboid, Triangular Prism, Rectangular Pyramid.

10 . A train is running at an average speed of 80 km per hour. It is covering up 4 km 4 m more in every interval of 10 minutes than that of a car. Find the average speed of the car.

11 . All the English alphabets are replaced by numbers from 1 to 26. In this way 1 stands for A, 3 for C and so on.

Decode the given message on the basis of above code.

    9   12 15 22 5   13 25 9 14 4 9 1

_______   ________   ______ ________

12. What least number must be added to 101,090,809 to make the number a multiple of 4?

13. Three angles of a triangle are in such a way that first angle is half of the second and one third of the third. Find all the three angles.

14. The floor of a room a hotel is 12 m long and 10 m wide. 45 tiles of 1 m square each was in stock. Tiles come in market in pack of ten tiles. How many more 1m square tiles does the manager need to completely cover the floors of three such rooms?
    I: 15 tiles more than 30 full pack
    II: 5 tiles more than 31 full pack
    III: 25 tiles more than 29 full pack
    IV: 50 tiles more than 25 full pack
    Select your answers: A: Only I   B: Only II   C: I, II and III   D: Only IV

15 . Mr. Jordon prepares to put fencing around his rectangular kitchen garden of width 95 m and the length 105 m. How long fencing wires does he need?
    A: 190 m B: 200 m   C: 210 m   D: 400 m

16. A half filled oil container is used to store residue oil of capacity 125 litters. After filling the residue three eighth of the container remained empty. Find the capacity of the container.

17. One tenth of a container is equal to 16 cans of capacity 8 litters each. The entire container can hold ___________ litters of oil.

18: What least number must be subtracted from 219.376 to make the result exactly divisible by 219?   [Ans: 0.157]

19: A train, moving at the speed of 15 m per second, is taking 20 seconds to cross a telephone post. This train can take ________ seconds to cross a 1.5 km long platform.
               [Ans : 2 minutes]

20: There are ________ diagonals in a pentagon.

21: A three digit greatest number is divisible by both 3 and 6. This number is also divisible by ________. This number must be an _______________ number.

22: A teacher purchased three types of pens.
     6 boxes of red pens with 40 pens in each box
     5 boxes of blue pens with 20 pens in each box
     Which number is closest to the total pens?
     A: 250   B: 350   C: 400   D: 450

Aid Box 1….

Match each exercise to its estimated sum or difference in the box.

1. $\frac{1}{5} + \frac{8}{9}$ 2. $\frac{6}{7} + \frac{11}{12}$

3. $\frac{9}{10} - \frac{5}{8}$ 4. $\frac{6}{13} - \frac{8}{18}$

a. $1 + 1 = 2$ b. $1 - \frac{1}{2} = \frac{1}{2}$

c. $\frac{1}{2} - \frac{1}{2} = 0$ d. $0 + 1 = 1$

Estimate the sum or difference.

5. $\frac{1}{11} + \frac{4}{9}$ 6. $\frac{15}{16} - \frac{1}{10}$ 7. $\frac{2}{9} + \frac{5}{6}$ 8. $\frac{11}{12} + \frac{12}{14}$

9. $\frac{7}{15} - \frac{1}{10}$ 10. $\frac{18}{20} - \frac{13}{24}$ 11. $\frac{3}{11} - \frac{1}{6}$ 12. $\frac{1}{9} + \frac{4}{10}$

13. $\frac{9}{10} + \frac{1}{6} + \frac{3}{8}$ 14. $\frac{1}{9} + \frac{1}{7} + \frac{1}{2}$ 15. $\frac{15}{16} + \frac{5}{8} + \frac{4}{9} + \frac{3}{25}$

16. $\frac{11}{12} + \frac{12}{14} + \frac{5}{8} + \frac{4}{9} + \frac{3}{25} + \frac{5}{6} + \frac{5}{6} + \frac{5}{6}$

17: Simplify: $\left(\frac{1}{2} + \frac{2}{4} + \frac{3}{6} + \cdots \cdots \frac{1001}{2002}\right) \div 2\left(1 + \frac{1}{1000}\right)$

18: Observe the Prime Factorisations:

a) 121   =   1 X 11 X 11;
b) 144   =   1 X 12 X 12;
c) 169   =   1 X 13 X 13;
d) 101   =   1 X 101;
e) 196   =   1 X 14 X 14;
f) 225   =   1 X 15 X 15;

Statements:

I.   All the numbers displayed above are square numbers having only three factors.
II.   1 comes as a factor in the prime factorisation of all natural numbers.
III.   None of the numbers displayed above are prime numbers.
IV.   Number having only two factors, 1 and the number itself, is called a prime number.

Is there any wrong statement?

Options:

A: Only ! and II are wrong.   B: Only III and V are wrong.
C: Only III is wrong.   D: Only II, III and V are wrong.

19: The chart displayed below exhibits some of the related quadrilaterals as per their some common properties. Examine the relationships before going through options.

Statements:

    I.   Square is a special type of rectangle having length equal to its breadth and all the interior angles right angle.

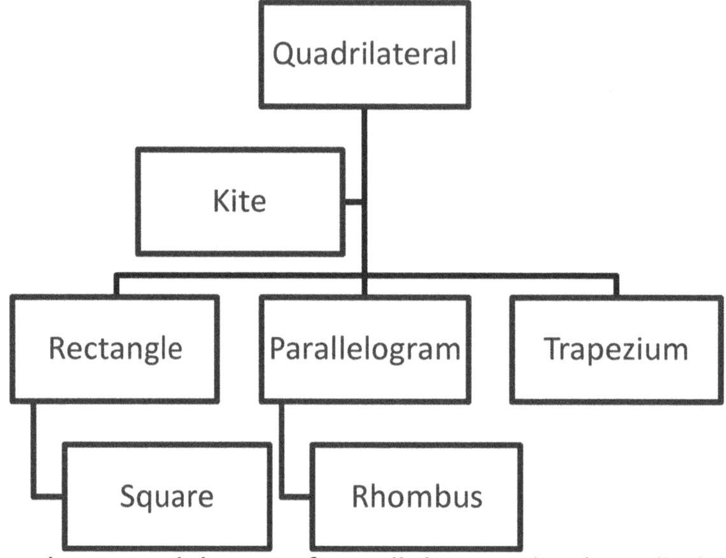

    II.   Rhombus is a special type of parallelogram having all sides equal to each other and opposite sides are parallel to each other.

    III.   Sum total of all the interior angles of each polygon displayed here is equal to two right angles.

    IV.   All these polygons are quadrilaterals as they all have 4 sides.

    V.   In this collection of polygons only square is a regular polygon.

Options:

A: Only III   B: Only IV   C: Only V   D: Only II

20: In a class of 40 students, $1/5^{th}$ of the total number of students like to eat rice only, $2/5^{th}$ of the total number of students like to eat bread only and the remaining students like to eat both. What fraction of the total number of students likes to eat both?

21: The directions for a pain reliever recommend that an adult of 60 kg and over can take 4 tablets every 4 hours as needed, and an adult who weighs between 40 and 50 kg take only2 and ½ tablets every 4 hours as needed. Each tablet weighs 4/25 gram.

a:If a 72 kg adult takes 4 tablets, how many grams of pain reliever is he or she receivings?

b: How many grams of pain reliever is the recommended dose for an adult weighing 46 kg?

Practice Papers

Paper I

Multiply. Look for patterns.

1. 18×10
   18×100
   18×1000
   $18 \times 10{,}000$

2. 40×5
   40×50
   40×500
   40×5000

3. 10×3.46
   100×3.46
   1000×3.46
   $10{,}000 \times 3.46$

Use rounding to estimate the product.

4. 37×88

5. 521×64

6. 23.2×9.18

Round to estimate. Then find each product.

7. 88×567

8. 3.05×2.3

9. 513×1901

10. $\$45.19 \times 140$

11. 6070×2820

12. 97.45×220

Write the standard form for each.

13. 5^2

14. 4^3

15. 6^0

16. 1^6

17. 2^5

18. Tap A can fill up a water tank in 30 minutes and tap B can empty the same water tank in 45 minutes. Tap A will take _____ minutes to fill the tank when both the taps remain open.

19. Two cubical block of edge 30 cm each joined side by side to form a cuboidal block. Find the surface area of the top and bottom part of that cuboid.

20: Malavika prepared a 25 m long rope by joining different segments of 200 cm each. Find the number of segments she used for making that rope.

21: _______ is the predecessor of smallest four digit multiple of 21.

22: A cistern can fill a water tank in 45 minutes and a tap can empty the same water tank in 1 hour 30 minutes. Find the time taken up by the cistern to fill the tank when the tap kept open.

23: Three triangles joined side by side to form a polygon having ___ sides. Sum total of all the interior angles of this polygon is _____ ^{0}.

24: Area of each white tiles in the pattern is 25 cm^2. White tiles are arranged in a uniform sequential pattern. Length of this shape is _________ cm, its breadth is _______ cm and area is __________ square cm.

Paper II

Divide using short division.

1. $3\overline{)81,993}$ 2. $6\overline{)84,174}$ 3. $5\overline{)490,135}$ 4. $7\overline{)315,714}$

5. $688,932 \div 4$ 6. $912,848 \div 8$ 7. $2,496,598 \div 2$ 8. $6,975,687 \div 3$

Predict if the quotient has a remainder. Explain why or why not. Then divide to check your prediction.

9. $5\overline{)509,845}$ 10. $3\overline{)68,734}$ 11. $2\overline{)149,568}$ 12. $3\overline{)710,625}$

Find each quotient by short division. Use R to write remainders.
Check by multiplying the divisor and the quotient
and then adding the remainder.

13. $4\overline{)137,973}$ 14. $9\overline{)836,138}$ 15. $5\overline{)139,864}$ 16. $7\overline{)180,523}$

17. $\$8157.75 \div 5$ 18. $\$644.68 \div 4$ 19. $36,570 \div 7$ 20. $19,580 \div 6$

21. A plot located in the front side of the residence of Mohan is rectangular in size. He has planted saplings in his front side plot at an interval of 2 m with uniformity in between 6 rows and 20 columns. Calculate the number of saplings Mohan arranged for this activity. Find the dimension of that plot.

22. The cost of tiling a square sized floor of side 6 m at the rate of Rs. 5 per square cm is Rs. __________.

23. A 1200 cm long wire is to be reshaped in rectangular form. Find the maximum possible and minimum possible length of that rectangle.

24. Mohan, Ravi, Kanika and Maneka are standing at four vertices of a rectangle having length 200 m and breadth 80 m. distance between Mohan and Ravi is greater than that of Kanika, but greatest distant from him is Maneka. Identify the types of intermediate distances in between these friends in terms of length, breadth and diagonals. Which of distances indicate diagonals of the rectangular shape?

25. What least number must be subtracted from 121.212 to make it divisible by 121?

26. Ravi purchased five dozens of banana at the rate of Rs 50 per dozen and sold them all at the rate of Rs 10 per pair. Calculate his gain or loss.

27. A wall mount clock strikes 2 bells in 2 seconds. This clock will take _______ seconds in striking 10 bells at 10 O'Clock.

28. Rita used half of the colours she had in stock. There were only 7 out of 12 poster colours in her stock. After using half of it what fraction of her stock left with her?

Paper III

Estimate Quotients:

1. $2164 \div 43$

2. $5838 \div 28$

3. $7842 \div 37$

4. $3984 \div 19$

5. $82,461 \div 41$

6. $\$51,206 \div 53$

7. $13,642 \div 206$

8. $85,136 \div 409$

9. $\$485,725 \div 520$

10. $672,385 \div 710$

11. $879,500 \div 425$

12. $\$972,360 \div 325$

Choose the best estimate.

13. $32\overline{)2940} \approx$ _?_   **a.** 1   **b.** 10   **c.** 100   **d.** 1000

14. $19\overline{)6248} \approx$ _?_   **a.** 3   **b.** 30   **c.** 300   **d.** 3000

15. $210\overline{)380,493} \approx$ _?_   **a.** 2   **b.** 20   **c.** 200   **d.** 2000

16. $389\overline{)792,432} \approx$ _?_   **a.** 2   **b.** 20   **c.** 200   **d.** 2000

17. Somalia distributed 11 and half cakes amongst her friends. Each friend got half of the slice. Find number of friends.

18. While dividing a greatest six digit even number by a common multiple of 2, 4, 8 and 24 the remainder received by Ponting is equal to P. Find value of $P^2 + 2P + 1$.

19. After dividing a natural number repeatedly by 5 for 3 times Soma got 202. Find the number.

20. The product of two numbers is 41310. If one of them is 270, find the other.

21. In certain division algorithm the quotient is 57, the divisor is 45 and the remainder is 29, find the dividend.

22: The annual income of Sam is Rs. 98,364. What is his monthly income if he earns an equal amount every month?

23: A number was divided by 97; the quotient was 3806 and the remainder 76. Find the number.

24: When 650 is multiplied by a number, the product is 5590. Find the number.

Paper IV

Write the missing term to complete the equivalent fraction.

3. $\dfrac{3}{4} = \dfrac{n}{12}$ 4. $\dfrac{1}{11} = \dfrac{a}{88}$ 5. $\dfrac{2}{9} = \dfrac{c}{81}$ 6. $\dfrac{2}{3} = \dfrac{q}{12}$ 7. $\dfrac{5}{7} = \dfrac{40}{f}$

8. $\dfrac{1}{8} = \dfrac{6}{b}$ 9. $\dfrac{1}{10} = \dfrac{3}{q}$ 10. $\dfrac{3}{11} = \dfrac{6}{s}$ 11. $\dfrac{9}{10} = \dfrac{r}{100}$ 12. $\dfrac{1}{25} = \dfrac{4}{d}$

13. $\dfrac{9}{30} = \dfrac{m}{10}$ 14. $\dfrac{4}{12} = \dfrac{t}{3}$ 15. $\dfrac{21}{28} = \dfrac{z}{4}$ 16. $\dfrac{40}{45} = \dfrac{x}{9}$ 17. $\dfrac{2}{6} = \dfrac{1}{h}$

18. $\dfrac{4}{k} = \dfrac{20}{25}$ 19. $\dfrac{6}{13} = \dfrac{24}{m}$ 20. $\dfrac{49}{e} = \dfrac{7}{8}$ 21. $\dfrac{x}{15} = \dfrac{36}{45}$ 22. $\dfrac{9}{16} = \dfrac{y}{144}$

Write two equivalent fractions for each fraction.

23. $\dfrac{5}{9}$ 24. $\dfrac{3}{5}$ 25. $\dfrac{1}{4}$ 26. $\dfrac{5}{10}$ 27. $\dfrac{6}{8}$

28. $\dfrac{3}{7}$ 29. $\dfrac{11}{15}$ 30. $\dfrac{9}{12}$ 31. $\dfrac{25}{75}$ 32. $\dfrac{8}{12}$

33: 49,000 fruits were distributed among 1,000 clubs equally. How many fruits did each club get?

34: Height of a pillar is increased by 5 m, 6 m and 7 m respectively to make it 6 m higher than another pillar of 20 m height. What was the previous height of that newly constructed pillar?

35: Mohan is two times older than Mohini who is again 5 years younger than Kavita. Kavita will be at her ten years next year. Find their ages.

36: Two sets of pillars counted by a visitor from standing in the middle. He has counted number of pillars from right hand side along with the pillar that he was holding as 10. From left hand side his counting in the same way was 9. How many pillars were there? Consider the fact that none of the pillars were identical.

37: Romanika counted a bundle of sheets, excluding that of top 15 ones, as 132. She has placed 21 sheets in to the printer. How many sheets were there in all?

38: Monika calculated 15th multiple of 5 added to 5th multiple of 15. Find the digit that she might have in the one's place of the product.

39: There are _______ flat faces and ____ curved faces in a cuboid.

Paper V

Write all the common factors for each set of numbers.

1. 8 and 24 **2.** 10 and 30 **3.** 15 and 35 **4.** 12 and 18

5. 16 and 20 **6.** 12 and 24 **7.** 30 and 18 **8.** 45 and 20

9. 4, 6, and 8 **10.** 6, 9, and 12 **11.** 5, 12, and 14 **12.** 6, 14, and 22

Find the GCF and the GCD of each set of numbers.

13. 6 and 12 **14.** 12 and 36 **15.** 8 and 10 **16.** 6 and 14

17. 9 and 30 **18.** 8 and 36 **19.** 24 and 42 **20.** 7 and 40

21. 8, 24, and 32 **22.** 5, 30, and 35 **23.** 15, 30, and 45

24: What least number should be subtracted from the six digit greatest number to make the value divisible by 3, 6, 9 and 18 independently leaving remainder 2 in each case?

25: 59 square shaped tiles each of 20 sq. cm. are used for   flooring a room. Find the area of that room.

26: Renuka prepared a bar graph that shows the number of kg of food eaten each day by each animal. What information goes on the horizontal axis? What information can be placed on the vertical axis?

27: Tim lives in New Delhi. He prepares a line graph that shows the amount of LPG used in his home kitchen for a year. Will the line graph show any change throughout the year?

28: Martin wants to represent the data related to pets owned by his classmates. He makes a bar graph that shows the number of dogs owned by members of his class. If the smallest number is 1 and the largest number is 4, what interval should Jon use for representing the data scale in the graph?

29: Kim gathered information about the population of individual states of her country. If she prepares a bar graph of this data, what information will be displayed on the vertical axis? What information will be displayed on the horizontal axis?

30: What greatest factor can divide 125, 625, 1,250 and 2,500 exactly?

Paper VI

Write the word name for each mixed number.

1. $7\frac{1}{2}$ **2.** $8\frac{4}{5}$ **3.** $5\frac{1}{10}$ **4.** $22\frac{1}{8}$ **5.** $1\frac{1}{20}$ **6.** $11\frac{11}{12}$

Write as a mixed number.

7. eleven and one fourth

8. nine and nine tenths

9. sixteen and three fifths

10. thirty and two thirds

11. twenty and fifteen sixteenths

12. twenty-one and seven tenths

Express each mixed number as a fraction.

13. $4\frac{1}{4}$ **14.** $2\frac{1}{2}$ **15.** $1\frac{3}{8}$ **16.** $2\frac{1}{8}$ **17.** $3\frac{4}{5}$ **18.** $5\frac{2}{7}$

19. $1\frac{1}{9}$ **20.** $1\frac{1}{10}$ **21.** $11\frac{1}{3}$ **22.** $12\frac{1}{2}$ **23.** $15\frac{1}{4}$ **24.** $12\frac{2}{7}$

25. $1\frac{5}{8}$ **26.** $5\frac{2}{3}$ **27.** $8\frac{2}{9}$ **28.** $10\frac{4}{5}$ **29.** $7\frac{7}{8}$ **30.** $19\frac{5}{7}$

31. Dana has only 2 rupees coins in her hand, and Ajah has exactly the same number of 5 rupees coins and no other coins. Together they have a total of Rs. 210. How many coins is each person holding? Find their individual shares in the collection.

32: When 2 pieces of rope are placed end-to-end, they measure 40 meters in length. When the 2 pieces are laid side-by-side, one is 10 meters longer than the other. How long is each piece of rope? Show your work.

33: Find the value: $\frac{11}{144} \times \frac{12}{121} \times \frac{12}{49} \times \frac{11}{169} \times \frac{7}{10} \times \frac{7}{100} =$

34: The town newspaper is published every alternate day. One copy has 12 pages. Every alternate day 21,980 copies are printed. How many total pages are printed for all copies every month?   [Consider one month equal to 30 days]

35: Simplify: $x^2 + 5y^2 + 3xy + 6x - 7y + 8 - [\, 12x^2 - \{\, 14x^2 - 9y^2 + 4xy + 3x + 9 \,\} \,]$

36: The quotient of x by y added to product of x and y. Write the expression which is obtained.

37: What least number should be subtracted from six digit greatest common multiple of 3, 6, 9 and 18 to make the value a common multiple of 5 and 10?

38: Sum total of reciprocal of a number and half of the given number is equal to 5.1. Find sum total of 10th and 15th multiple of that number.

Paper VII

Compare. Write <, =, or >. You can use a number line to help.

1. $\frac{7}{8}$? $\frac{5}{8}$ 2. $\frac{9}{20}$? $\frac{9}{20}$ 3. $\frac{14}{30}$? $\frac{26}{30}$ 4. $\frac{17}{21}$? $\frac{10}{21}$

5. $\frac{12}{7}$? $\frac{16}{7}$ 6. $\frac{9}{8}$? $\frac{8}{8}$ 7. $\frac{22}{6}$? $\frac{32}{6}$ 8. $\frac{19}{19}$? $\frac{20}{19}$

Rename each pair of fractions using the LCD as their denominator.

9. $\frac{3}{5}$ and $\frac{1}{4}$ 10. $\frac{3}{4}$ and $\frac{1}{10}$ 11. $\frac{7}{8}$ and $\frac{5}{6}$ 12. $\frac{1}{2}$ and $\frac{2}{3}$

13. $\frac{1}{12}$ and $\frac{3}{24}$ 14. $\frac{1}{3}$ and $\frac{4}{9}$ 15. $\frac{5}{7}$ and $\frac{12}{49}$ 16. $\frac{2}{5}$ and $\frac{4}{7}$

Compare. Write <, =, or >. You can use a number line to help.

17. $\frac{1}{4}$? $\frac{7}{16}$ 18. $\frac{7}{10}$? $\frac{3}{5}$ 19. $\frac{4}{21}$? $\frac{1}{7}$ 20. $\frac{6}{14}$? $\frac{2}{7}$

21. $\frac{3}{5}$? $\frac{5}{8}$ 22. $\frac{4}{7}$? $\frac{6}{9}$ 23. $\frac{7}{12}$? $\frac{9}{15}$ 24. $\frac{10}{25}$? $\frac{7}{10}$

25: Somalia converted six digit greatest multiple of 4 into a common multiple of 5, 10 and 15 by subtracting ……………. from it. (Consider it as a smallest possible number.).

26: Is there any pair of number having LCM 12321 and HCF 1690?

27: What least number can be subtracted from the greatest even number of six digits to obtain a multiple of 6?

28: Sum total of five consecutive numbers is equal to third multiple 150,005. Find sum total of smallest and greatest numbers of this number series.

29: Rohit can finish half of a wall painting in 12 days and Mohan can finish quarter of the same painting in 4 days. They started working jointly to finish 7 such wall paintings. They can finish their works in ……….. days.

30: A train can cross a light post in 1 m 4 seconds while moving with a uniform speed of 72 km/h. Find time to be taken by this train to cross a tunnel of length 5 km 60 m.

31: Sneha reduced her consumption of fuel by 20% to balance price rise of fuel. Calculate the percentage increase of cost of fuel by using the above data.

32: After incorporating Joseph in a team of 11 students of average height 1 m 6 cm the average age is increased by 12 cm. Find height of John.

Paper VIII

The number line shows that $\frac{2}{3} < 1\frac{1}{4} < 1\frac{5}{6}$.

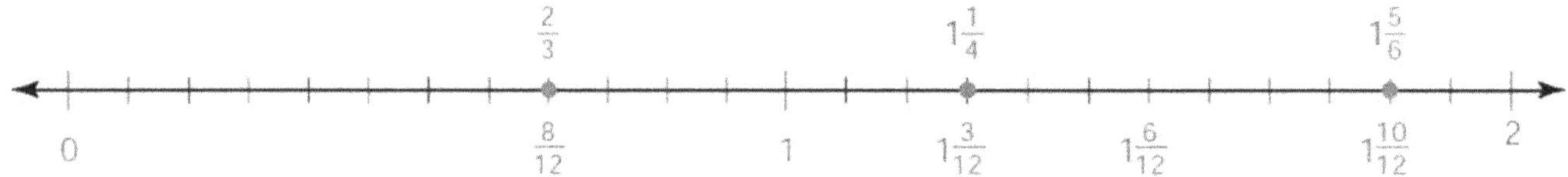

From least to greatest: $\frac{2}{3}$, $1\frac{1}{4}$, $1\frac{5}{6}$

From greatest to least: $1\frac{5}{6}$, $1\frac{1}{4}$, $\frac{2}{3}$

Study these examples.

Order from greatest to least.

$2\frac{1}{8}$, $2\frac{3}{4}$, $\frac{19}{8}$

$\downarrow$ $\downarrow$ $\downarrow$

$2\frac{1}{8}$, $2\frac{6}{8}$, $2\frac{3}{8}$

$\frac{19}{8} = 8\overline{)19}\;\;\overset{2\frac{3}{8}}{}$

From greatest to least: $2\frac{3}{4}$, $\frac{19}{8}$, $2\frac{1}{8}$

$6\frac{5}{6}$, $6\frac{3}{5}$, $6\frac{2}{3}$

$\downarrow$ $\downarrow$ $\downarrow$

$6\frac{25}{30}$, $6\frac{18}{30}$, $6\frac{20}{30}$

LCD is 30.

From greatest to least: $6\frac{5}{6}$, $6\frac{2}{3}$, $6\frac{3}{5}$

Write in order from least to greatest.

1. $\frac{4}{5}$, $\frac{7}{10}$, $\frac{3}{4}$

2. $\frac{5}{12}$, $\frac{3}{8}$, $\frac{5}{6}$

3. $9\frac{3}{5}$, $9\frac{5}{8}$, $9\frac{7}{10}$

4. $7\frac{2}{9}$, $7\frac{1}{3}$, $7\frac{3}{4}$

Write in order from greatest to least.

5. $\frac{7}{12}$, $\frac{1}{2}$, $\frac{2}{3}$

6. $\frac{1}{4}$, $\frac{1}{3}$, $\frac{1}{5}$

7. $\frac{2}{5}$, $\frac{7}{10}$, $\frac{1}{3}$

8. $\frac{7}{12}$, $\frac{4}{5}$, $\frac{9}{10}$

9. $5\frac{4}{5}$, $5\frac{3}{4}$, $5\frac{7}{8}$

10. $2\frac{2}{3}$, $3\frac{3}{4}$, $2\frac{4}{5}$

11. $\frac{17}{18}$, $\frac{7}{9}$, $\frac{2}{3}$

12. $\frac{3}{7}$, $\frac{1}{2}$, $\frac{3}{14}$

13. $\frac{21}{9}$, $\frac{12}{9}$, $\frac{9}{12}$

14. $\frac{7}{6}$, $\frac{14}{5}$, $\frac{31}{10}$

15. $1\frac{2}{15}$, $\frac{18}{15}$, $1\frac{4}{15}$

16. $\frac{21}{9}$, $1\frac{5}{9}$, $\frac{8}{3}$

17: Half of a quarter of 16,064 + one seventh of 14,056 + 1/11th of 22,088 = ...

18: Simplify: $\left(1 + \frac{1}{11}\right)\left(1 + \frac{1}{12}\right) .... \left(1 + \frac{1}{1,000}\right) \div 2,002 \, X \, 121 - 101$ = ...

19: Fifty times 5,050 divided by one fifth of 175 = ...

20: Half of one seventh of 560,070 − 400,005 = ...

Paper IX

Fractions and mixed numbers with denominators that are *powers of ten* can be renamed as decimals. The word names are the same.

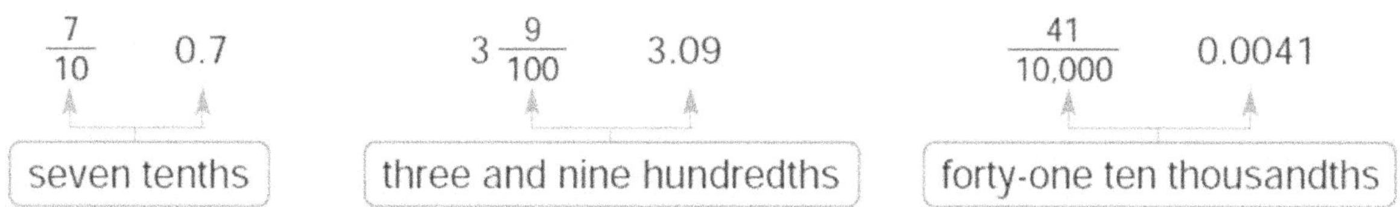

$$\frac{7}{10} \qquad 0.7 \qquad\qquad 3\frac{9}{100} \qquad 3.09 \qquad\qquad \frac{41}{10,000} \qquad 0.0041$$

| seven tenths | three and nine hundredths | forty-one ten thousandths |

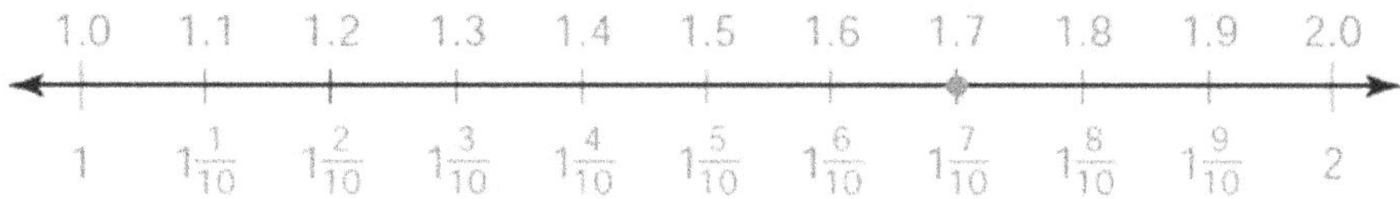

1.7, $\frac{17}{10}$, and $1\frac{7}{10}$ all have the same value.
They all name one and seven tenths.

Writing decimal as fraction:

- Write an equivalent fraction. $\qquad$ thirty-five hundredths $= \dfrac{35}{100}$

- Simplify if necessary. $\qquad \dfrac{35}{100} = \dfrac{35 \div 5}{100 \div 5} = \dfrac{7}{20}$

So $0.35 = \dfrac{7}{20}$.

Study this example.

Write 9.008 as a mixed number in simplest form.

$$9.008 \longrightarrow \text{nine and eight thousandths} \longrightarrow 9\frac{8}{1000}$$

$$\frac{8}{1000} = \frac{8 \div 8}{1000 \div 8} = \frac{1}{125}$$

1: Convert the following expression into an equivalent fraction.

a: 20 tenths + 203 hundredths + 2,005 thousandths + 12 tenths

b: 15/19th of 19,019 + 11/13th of 13,013 + 16/33rd of 33,033 = ………………

c: Half of 500 multiplied by 625 and again multiplied by 1,000

2: Sum total of a number and its reciprocal is equal to 8.125. Find the number.

Paper X

1: What fraction of all the numbers starting from 1 to 1,000 are multiples of 25?

2: Write three fractions which can be placed in between 1/3 and ¼ on a number line.

3. Half of a quarter of a number exceeds eighth multiple of 300,003 by 72. Find the number.

4: Radius of a square sized playground is equal to 21 m. Mohini completes her daily practice of jogging by encircling around it for four times. Find total distance covered by Mohini during her daily jogging.

5: A cistern can fill up a water tank in 45 minutes another cistern takes 1 h 30 m to fill up the same water tank. Both the tanks kept open to fill up the water tank. Time taken by both the cisterns jointly to fill up the water tank will be …………………..

6: Simplify: [(5.5 + 5.05 + 5.005 + 5.0005 + 5.00005 + 5.000005) − 25] ÷ 5 = …………………

7: Cost of half a dozen banana is equal to Rs 40. Cost of 50 bananas will be Rs. ………………

8: Rijuana travels 20 m in a couple of seconds by using her car. Mohini travels by using her car with an average speed of 76 km/h. They started jointly from the origin and a gap developed in between them after half an hour. Calculate the gap developed in between them as they were travelling in the same direction.

9: Calculate the least possible time interval after which three bells toll together. These bells toll at an interval of 10 seconds, 15 seconds and 20 seconds respectively.

Write each decimal as a fraction in simplest form.

10. 0.9	11. 0.07	12. 0.43	13. 0.77	14. 0.003
15. 0.127	16. 0.45	17. 0.36	18. 0.675	19. 0.325
20. 0.0033	21. 0.0009	22. 0.441	23. 0.101	24. 0.0500

Write each decimal as a mixed number in simplest form.

25. 1.09	26. 5.7	27. 11.31	28. 12.1	29. 2.5
30. 8.4	31. 9.16	32. 6.35	33. 1.055	34. 3.004
35. 6.0005	36. 8.0010	37. 3.375	38. 2.95	39. 20.0750

40: What fraction of all the numbers from 1 to 550 are multiples of 11?

41: Is there any pair of number having LCM 1210 and HCF 625?

42: In her social studies report, Suzanne included a bar graph that showed the populations of different Native American nations in 1800. The interval she used was 2,000 people. If one nation had a population represented by 2.5 intervals, how many members of this nation existed in 1800?

Paper XI

Rewrite each repeating decimal with a bar over the part that repeats.

1. 0.66666 . . .   **2.** 0.11111 . . .   **3.** 0.45454 . . .   **4.** 0.09090 . . .

5. 0.83333 . . .   **6.** 0.26666 . . .   **7.** 2.384848 . . .   **8.** 5.13232 . . .

Write each repeating decimal showing eight decimal places.

9. $0.\overline{1}$ **10.** $0.\overline{12}$ **11.** $0.1\overline{4}$ **12.** $0.2\overline{8}$

13. $5.\overline{3}$ **14.** $12.\overline{06}$ **15.** $7.2\overline{7}$ **16.** $13.2\overline{17}$

Rename each fraction as a terminating or repeating decimal.

17. $\frac{1}{8}$ **18.** $\frac{13}{20}$ **19.** $\frac{5}{11}$ **20.** $\frac{1}{3}$ **21.** $\frac{3}{4}$

22. $\frac{2}{9}$ **23.** $\frac{7}{16}$ **24.** $\frac{5}{12}$ **25.** $\frac{11}{18}$ **26.** $\frac{1}{16}$

27: Simplify: (1.111…. + 2.222…… + 3.33…..+ 4.444…….) – 10 = ………………

28: Anthony emptied his coin bank and made a bar graph of the numbers of each type of coin. The interval he chose was 5 coins. If the graph showed 5 intervals of quarters, 2 intervals of dimes, 3 intervals of nickels, and 10 intervals of pennies, what was the total amount of money in his bank?

29: The floor of a room a hotel is 12 m long and 10 m wide. 45 tiles of 1 m square was in stock. Tiles come in market in pack of ten tiles. How many more 1m square tiles does the manager need to completely cover the floors of three such rooms?

I: 15 tiles more than 30 full pack   II: 5 tiles more than 31 full pack

III: 25 tiles more than 29 full pack   IV: 50 tiles more than 25 full pack

Select your answers

A: Only I   B: Only II   C: I, II and III   D: Only IV

30: Average of ten consecutive even numbers is 20. Is it possible to work out values of all the numbers? Find the average of first six such numbers.

31. Instead of adding 108, Ravi subtracted 100.81 from a collection of 50 find the difference of the desired result and wrong result.

32: Sum total of all the even numbers starting from 2 to 10,000 is __________________.

Paper XII

Identify the rational number that corresponds to the point on the number line.

1. *C*　　　2. *F*　　　3. *A*　　　4. *E*　　　5. *B*　　　6. *D*

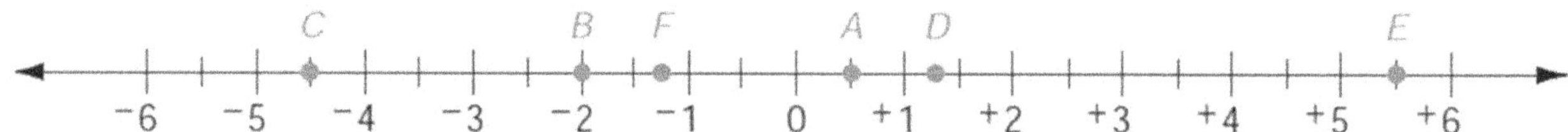

Write a rational number for each point.

7.　8.

9.　10.

11.　12.

13.　14.

15: Consider all the four digit numbers formed by using digits 8, 4, 7 and 0. If you arrange these numbers in descending orders then _______a_______ comes in the second position and ___b___ comes at last.

A: a =8,470 b = 4,078,　　　　　　B: a= 8,740, b= 4,087

C: a =8,470 b = 4,078;　　　　　　D: a = 8,740 b = 4087

16: Anamika prepares to put fencing around her rectangular kitchen garden of width 95.24 m and the length 105 m 76 cm. How long fencing wires does she need to cover the entire outer boundary leaving a 3 m broad entrance open?

A: 400 m 200　　　B: 399 m　　C: 202 m 2 cm　　　　D: 397.2 m

17: At 10 O' Clock and 2 O' Click both hour hand and minute hand of a clock makes an angle of ___a_____ which is __b__ of its complementary angle and ___c___of its supplementary angle.

A: a= 900　　b = 1/4th　　c = 4/5th　　　　B: a= 1800　　b = 1/2nd　　c = 2/3rd

C: a= 2700　　b = 1/3rd　　c = 3/4th　　　　D: a= 600　　b = double　　c = 1/2.

Paper XIII

Compute mentally. Find the whole-number part and then the fraction part.

1. $8\frac{2}{3} - 5\frac{1}{3}$

2. $6\frac{7}{8} - 2\frac{5}{8}$

3. $10\frac{1}{12} + 1\frac{7}{12}$

4. $12\frac{1}{16} + 8\frac{7}{16}$

5. $10\frac{3}{8} - 4\frac{1}{8} + 2$

6. $9\frac{7}{15} - 3\frac{2}{15} - 4$

Compute mentally. Look for sums of 1.

7. $6\frac{1}{3} + 8\frac{2}{3} + 7$

8. $2\frac{3}{8} + 1\frac{5}{8}$

9. $5\frac{1}{4} + 1\frac{1}{4} + \frac{1}{2}$

10. $1\frac{1}{16} + 5\frac{1}{2} + 2\frac{3}{16} + 2\frac{1}{4}$

11. $3\frac{1}{12} + 7\frac{7}{12} + 8\frac{1}{3}$

12. $3\frac{1}{3} + 6\frac{4}{5} + 10\frac{2}{3} + 3\frac{1}{5}$

13. $9\frac{3}{4} + 5\frac{6}{11} + 6\frac{1}{4}$

Compensate to compute mentally.

14. $8 - 4\frac{1}{3}$

15. $12 - 10\frac{5}{6}$

16. $5\frac{1}{3} - \frac{2}{3}$

17: What fraction of all the numbers starting from 1 to 63 are multiples of 3?

18: Simplify: $\left[1{,}502 - \left(\frac{1}{2} + \frac{2}{4} + \frac{3}{6} + \frac{4}{8} + \cdots \ldots \frac{1002}{2004}\right) \right] X \left(1 + \frac{1}{1{,}000}\right)$

19: Find the least number which can be subtracted from six didit greatest multiple of 4 to obtain a common multiple of 2, 4 and 11.

20: $(1 + 2 + 3 + \ldots\ldots + 500) \div 501 \, X \, 250 \, X \, 16 = 10^{P}$; find the value of $(P^{3} + 2P^{2} + 100P)$

21: Sum total of five consecutive number is equal to 10,000. Find all the numbers.

22: Express each of the following numbers using exponential notation:

(i) 512,00　　　　(ii) 343,000　　　　(iii) 729,000　(iv) 3125　　(v) 12321

23: Simplify:
(i) $(-4)^{3}$　　　(ii) $(-3) \, X \, (-2)^{3}$　　　(iii) $(-3)^{2} \, X \, (-5)^{2} \, X \, (-5)^{2}$　　　　　(iv) $(-2)^{3} \, X \, (-10)^{3}$

24: State whether the following ratios are proportional or not:

(i) 20 : 45 and 4 : 9　　　　(ii) 9 : 27 and 33 : 11

Paper XIV

Evaluate:

1. $5\frac{1}{2} + n$, when $n = 3\frac{1}{4}$

2. $7\frac{1}{8} - y$, when $y = 0$

3. $1\frac{1}{6} + r + 1\frac{2}{5}$, when $r = 1\frac{3}{4}$

4. $k - 10\frac{1}{10} + 0$, when $k = 14\frac{2}{3}$

5. $9\frac{1}{6} + \frac{5}{6} - m$, when $m = \frac{1}{2}$

6. $1\frac{1}{2} + s + 6\frac{3}{4}$, when $s = 1\frac{3}{8}$

7. $f - 1\frac{3}{5} + g$, when $f = 2\frac{1}{4}$ and $g = 5\frac{1}{2}$

8. $5 + 3\frac{3}{8} + d + 2\frac{5}{8}$, when $d = 6\frac{1}{6}$

Simplify each expression. Use mental math and the properties of addition.

9. $5\frac{2}{5} + 3\frac{3}{5} + 6\frac{1}{4}$

10. $8\frac{1}{8} + 4\frac{1}{4} + 5\frac{7}{8}$

11. $0 + 11\frac{2}{5}$

12. $9\frac{1}{6} + 0$

13. $7\frac{1}{2} + 6 + 4\frac{1}{4}$

14. $3\frac{3}{4} + 2\frac{1}{2} + 11$

15. $12\frac{1}{4} + 5\frac{1}{8} + 2\frac{1}{2}$

16. $9\frac{1}{2} + 4\frac{3}{7} + 1\frac{1}{4}$

17. $(\frac{1}{2} + 2\frac{3}{5}) + 1\frac{1}{2}$

18. $8\frac{1}{4} + (4\frac{1}{9} + \frac{3}{4})$

19: $\left[10{,}002 - \left(1\frac{1}{2} + 1\frac{2}{4} + 1\frac{3}{6} + \cdots .. 1\frac{10{,}002}{20{,}004}\right)\right]$

20: 240, 360, x are in continued proportion, find the value of x.

21: Sum total of a number and its reciprocal is equal to 8.125. Find the number.

22: What least number should be subtracted from the greatest six digit common multiple of 2, 4 and 8 to obtain a common multiple of 3. 5 and 10?

23: Rijuana spends 7 days to finish a work while working 9 hours a day. Pinki spends 9 days to finish the same work while working 7 hours a day. They jointly started working in a couple of similar project while working 7 hours a day. Calculate duration of their project activity as they continued working jointly.

24: A wall munt clock takes 4 seconds for striking 4 bells at 4 p.m. What time will be taken by that clock for striking 10 bells at 10 p.m?

25: Rikin can finish a work in 24 days while working 7 hours a day. He can finish the same work in …….. days while working 8 hours per day.

Paper XV

Evaluate:

1. $\dfrac{5}{9} + \dfrac{3}{7}$ **2.** $\dfrac{14}{15} - \dfrac{7}{8}$ **3.** $9\dfrac{1}{6} - 7\dfrac{1}{2}$ **4.** $12\dfrac{9}{10} + 11\dfrac{6}{7}$

Add or subtract. Estimate to help.

5. $\dfrac{1}{2}$ **6.** $4\dfrac{1}{8}$ **7.** $\dfrac{1}{3}$ **8.** $4\dfrac{5}{7}$ **9.** 5 **10.** 10

$+\dfrac{1}{3}$ $+6\dfrac{3}{8}$ $-\dfrac{1}{4}$ $-1\dfrac{2}{7}$ $-1\dfrac{1}{2}$ $-2\dfrac{3}{4}$

11. $14\dfrac{3}{10} - 1\dfrac{1}{3}$ **12.** $1\dfrac{3}{8} + 19\dfrac{2}{3}$ **13.** $10 - 1\dfrac{1}{10}$ **14.** $4\dfrac{3}{7} - 1\dfrac{1}{6}$

15. $4\dfrac{1}{4} + 1\dfrac{1}{2} + 2\dfrac{3}{8}$ **16.** $\dfrac{1}{8} + 3\dfrac{2}{3} + 3\dfrac{7}{8}$ **17.** $15\dfrac{3}{8} - 9\dfrac{7}{8}$

Compute. Use mental math and the properties of addition.

18. $\dfrac{1}{4} + \dfrac{1}{4}$ **19.** $5\dfrac{1}{6} + (3\dfrac{1}{2} - 3\dfrac{1}{2})$ **20.** $7\dfrac{1}{4} + 3\dfrac{1}{2}$

Evaluate each expression for the given values.

21. $7\dfrac{3}{8} - n$, when $n = 3\dfrac{1}{8}$ **22.** $r + 5\dfrac{1}{3} + 2\dfrac{3}{5}$, when $r = 1\dfrac{2}{5}$

23: Find Area…

(i)
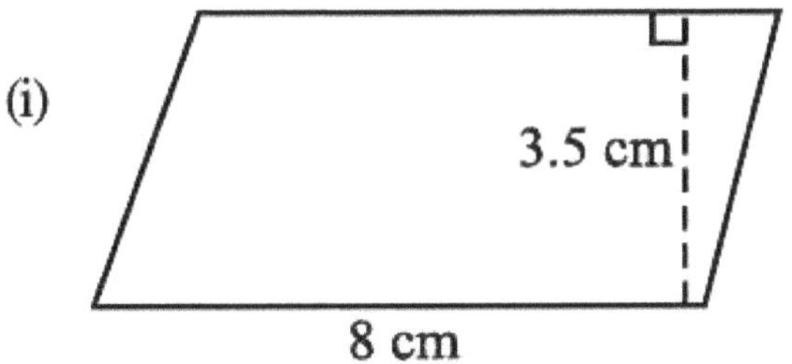

(ii)
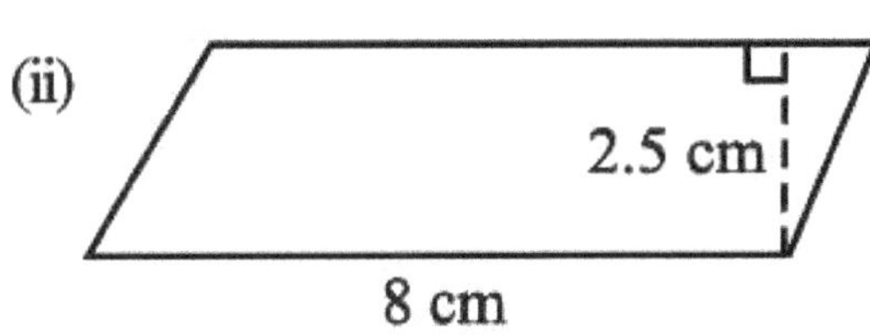

(iii) In a parallelogram ABCD, AB = 7.2 cm and the perpendicular from C on AB is 4.5 cm.

24: A circular flower garden has an area of 314 m². A sprinkler placed at the centre of the garden can cover an area that has a radius of 12 m. Will the sprinkler irrigate the entire garden effectively? (Take pi = 3.14)

15. Find the circumference of the inner and the outer circles. Radiuses of both the concentric circles are 21 cm and 14 cm respectively. Also find the area carved out by both the circles.

Paper XVI

Add or subtract. Estimate to help you.

1. $\dfrac{7}{12} + \dfrac{13}{24}$
2. $\dfrac{5}{6} - \dfrac{1}{5}$
3. $2\dfrac{1}{5} + 4\dfrac{3}{5}$
4. $9\dfrac{5}{7} - 8\dfrac{2}{7}$

5. $8\dfrac{3}{5} + 6\dfrac{1}{3}$
6. $5\dfrac{5}{7} + 4$
7. $4\dfrac{3}{8} - 1\dfrac{1}{7}$

8. $1\dfrac{1}{2} + 2\dfrac{1}{3} + 1\dfrac{5}{6}$
9. $12 - 1\dfrac{1}{8}$
10. $15\dfrac{9}{10} - 14\dfrac{1}{3}$

Compute. Use the addition properties when possible.

11. $2\dfrac{4}{5} + (1\dfrac{1}{3} - 1\dfrac{1}{3})$
12. $(\dfrac{1}{4} + 5\dfrac{3}{8}) + 3\dfrac{3}{4}$
13. $2\dfrac{1}{2} + 4 + 1\dfrac{1}{4}$

Evaluate each expression for the given values.

14. $2\dfrac{5}{6} - n$, when $n = 1\dfrac{1}{2}$
15. $4\dfrac{5}{8} + c + 2\dfrac{1}{8}$, when $c = 1\dfrac{2}{5}$

Solve and check.

16. $a + \dfrac{1}{4} = \dfrac{1}{2}$
17. $t + 1\dfrac{1}{2} = 3\dfrac{1}{2}$
18. $n - \dfrac{3}{8} = \dfrac{5}{16}$

Observe the example:

The two sides of the parallelogram ABCD are 6 cm and 4 cm. The height corresponding to the base CD is 3 cm . Find the

(i) area of the parallelogram. (ii) the height corresponding to the base AD.

Solution

(i) Area of parallelogram $= b \times h$

$$= 6 \text{ cm} \times 3 \text{ cm} = 18 \text{ cm}^2$$

(ii) base $(b) = 4$ cm, height $= x$ (say),

$$\text{Area} = 18 \text{ cm}^2$$

Area of parallelogram $= b \times x$

$$18 = 4 \times x$$

$$\dfrac{18}{4} = x$$

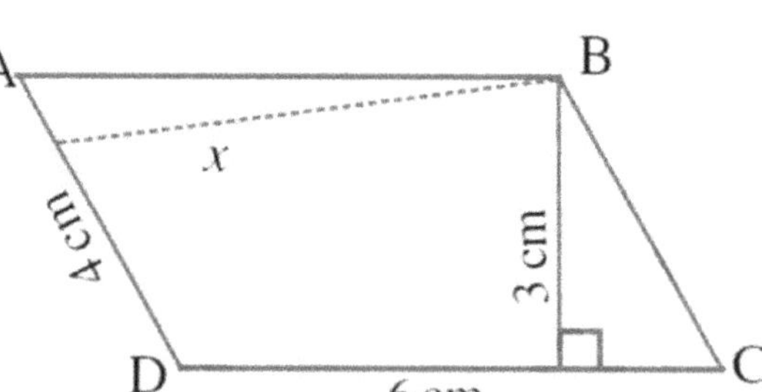

Therefore, $x = 4.5$ cm

Thus, the height corresponding to base AD is 4.5 cm.

On the basis of the example solve the following:

1. Find the area of each of the following parallelograms:

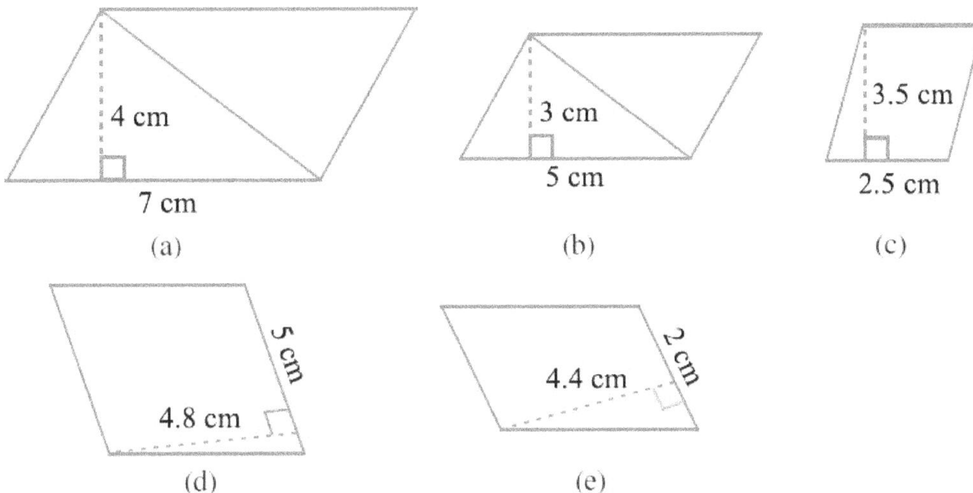

2. Find the area of each of the following triangles:

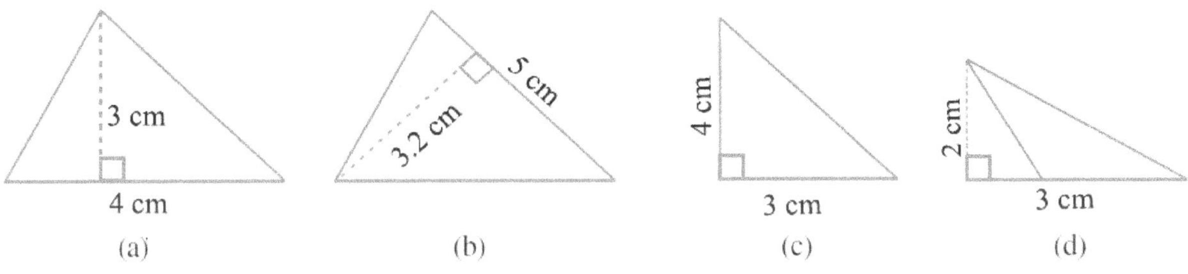

3. Find the missing values:

S.No.	Base	Height	Area of the Parallelogram
a.	20 cm		246 cm^2
b.		15 cm	154.5 cm^2
c.		8.4 cm	48.72 cm^2
d.	15.6 cm		16.38 cm^2

19: A circle of radius 2 cm is cut out from a square piece of an aluminium sheet of side 6 cm. What is the area of the left over aluminium sheet?

20: A pentagon can have at least …… unique diagonals.

21: Five squares each of side 15 cm are arranged side by side to form a longest possible rectangle of length ……. cm.

Paper XVII

1. If $m = 2$, find the value of:

    (i) $m - 2$ (ii) $3m - 5$ (iii) $9 - 5m$

    (iv) $3m^2 - 2m - 7$ (v) $\dfrac{5m}{2}\ 4$

2. If $p = -2$, find the value of:

    (i) $4p + 7$ (ii) $-3p^2 + 4p + 7$ (iii) $-2p^3 - 3p^2 + 4p + 7$

3. Find the value of the following expressions, when $x = -1$:

    (i) $2x - 7$ (ii) $-x + 2$ (iii) $x^2 + 2x + 1$

    (iv) $2x^2 - x - 2$

4. If $a = 2, b = -2$, find the value of:

    (i) $a^2 + b^2$ (ii) $a^2 + ab + b^2$ (iii) $a^2 - b^2$

5. When $a = 0, b = -1$, find the value of the given expressions:

    (i) $2a + 2b$ (ii) $2a^2 + b^2 + 1$ (iii) $2a^2b + 2ab^2 + ab$

    (iv) $a^2 + ab + 2$

6. Simplify the expressions and find the value if x is equal to 2

(i) $x + 7 + 4(x - 5)$ (ii) $3(x + 2) + 5x - 7$

(iii) $6x + 5(x - 2)$ (iv) $4(2x - 1) + 3x + 11$

(v) $\left(\dfrac{1}{x} + \dfrac{2}{x} + \dfrac{3}{x} + \dfrac{4}{x} + \cdots \ldots \dfrac{2,000}{x}\right) \div \dfrac{2x^2}{1,000\,x^3} + \dfrac{5\,x}{300}$

7: What should be the value of a if the value of $2x^2 + x - a$ equals to 5, when x = 0?

8: Simlify the following for a = 3 and b = 4; $2(a^2 + ab) + 3 - ab + (a + b)^2$

9: The .... is the numerical factor in the term. Sometimes anyone factor in a term is called the coefficient of the remaining part of the term.

10: Terms which have the same algebraic factors are .... terms. Terms which have different algebraic factors are .... terms.

11: Convert the given decimal fractions to per cents.

(a) 0.65   (b) 2.1   (c) 0.02   (d) 12.35   (e) 0.625   (f) 1.125

12: What percent of all the natural numbers up to 1,250 are multiples of 125?

13: Find: (a) 15% of 2500 (b) 1% of 6% of 1 hour (c) 20% of `30% of 2500 (d) 75% of 1 kg

Appplication of Divisibility Rules

Numbers are divisible independently by its factors. Group of numbers are divisible by common factors.

Divisibility rules:

Divisible by	Rules
2	it is an even number (ends in 0, 2, 4, 6, or 8)
3	the sum of its digits is divisible by 3
4	the last two digits form a number divisible by 4
5	the ones digit is 0 or 5
6	it is divisible by both 2 and 3
8	the last three digits form a number divisible by 8
9	the sum of its digits is divisible by 9
10	the last digit is 0

Study this example.

Determine whether 3024 is divisible by 2, 3, 4, 5, 6, 8, 9, and/or 10.

3024 → 4 is an even number.	3024 is divisible by 2.
3024 → 3 + 0 + 2 + 4 = 9 and 9 ÷ 3 = 3	3024 is divisible by 3.
3024 → 24 ÷ 4 = 6	3024 is divisible by 4.
3024 → 4 is not 0 or 5.	3024 is *not* divisible by 5.
3024 → 4 is an even number and 3 + 0 + 2 + 4 = 9 and 9 ÷ 3 = 3.	3024 is divisible by 6.
3024 → 24 ÷ 8 = 3	3024 is divisible by 8.
3024 → 3 + 0 + 2 + 4 = 9 and 9 ÷ 9 = 1	3024 is divisible by 9.
3024 → 4 is not 0.	3024 is *not* divisible by 10.

So 3024 is divisible by 2, 3, 4, 6, 8, and 9.

Similarly check divisibility of following numbers:

1. 333	**2.** 128	**3.** 225	**4.** 7535	**5.** 8289
6. 9410	**7.** 99,483	**8.** 67,704	**9.** 67,713	**10.** 67,722
11. 23,918	**12.** 35,932	**13.** 85,446	**14.** 40,620	**15.** 90,990
16. 17,934	**17.** 49,708	**18.** 77,075	**19.** 13,104	**20.** 486,890
21. 207,984	**22.** 352,860	**23.** 607,712	**24.** 581,889	**25.** 270,228

Find the missing digit or digits that would make each number divisible by the given number.

26. 3,95☐; by 10

> **Think**
> The last digit must be **0** to be divisible by 10.

27. 17,84☐; by 3

28. 243,05☐; by 9

29. 698,39☐; by 3 and by 9

30. 17,39☐; by 5

31. 14,5☐2; by 8

32. 13,☐12; by 8 and by 3

33. 27,1☐8; by 6

34. 20,71☐; by 4

35. 502,7☐5; by 3 and by 5

36. 37,6☐3; by 9

37. 98☐,124; by 6

38. 109,83☐; by 4 and by 8

Tell whether each number is *prime, composite,* or *neither.*

39. 24   40. 35   41. 2   **42.** 9   43. 19
44. 21   45. 33   46. 11   47. 101   48. **1**.002
49. 51   50. 26   51. 81   52. 100   53. 41
54. 207   55. 613   56. 127   57. 10,011   58. 37,311

Prime Factorisation ....

Find the prime factorization of 9450.

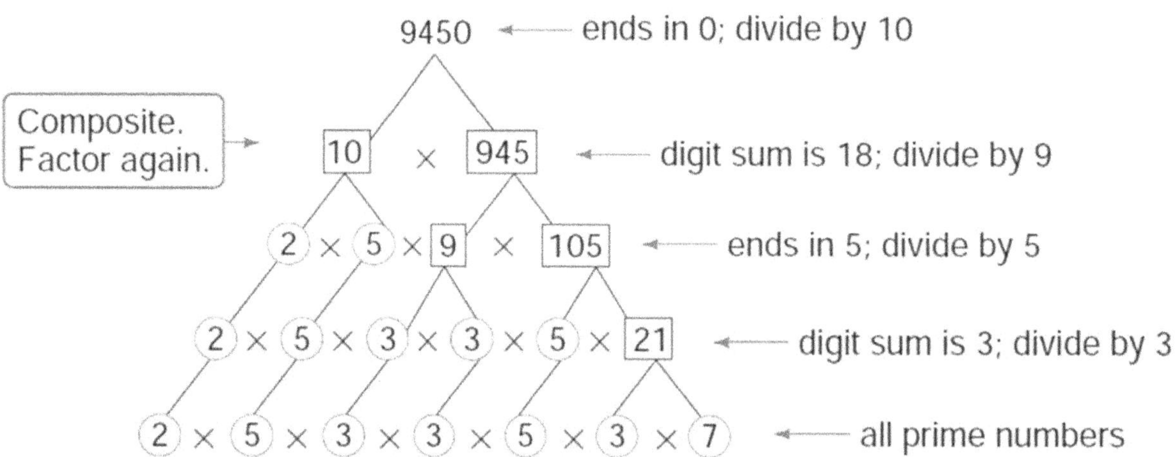

So, the prime factorization of 9450 is $2 \times 3^3 \times 5^2 \times 7$.

Prepare Prime Factorisation diagram for the following:

59. 95   60. 114   61. 153   62. 390   63. 504

64. 189   65. 225   66. 540   67. 1215   68. 2916

***.

Orders of Operations

Remember the order of operations: 1. Grouping Symbols; 2. Exponents; 3. Multiply or divide from left to right; 4. Add or subtract from left to right.

This order of operation is also coined as follows:

    Bracket   Of   Division   Multiplication Addition   Subtraction

Let us work out a mathematical statement for the following:

A shark descends 6 feet from the surface of the ocean. Then it descends 15 more feet. It repeats this dive two more times. After the three dives, the whale ascends 36 feet. How many feet below the surface is the shark then?

Mathematical statement for this problem is: $[-6 + 3 \times (-15) + 36] = -15$;

The shark is -15 feet below the surface.

Consider two more examples:

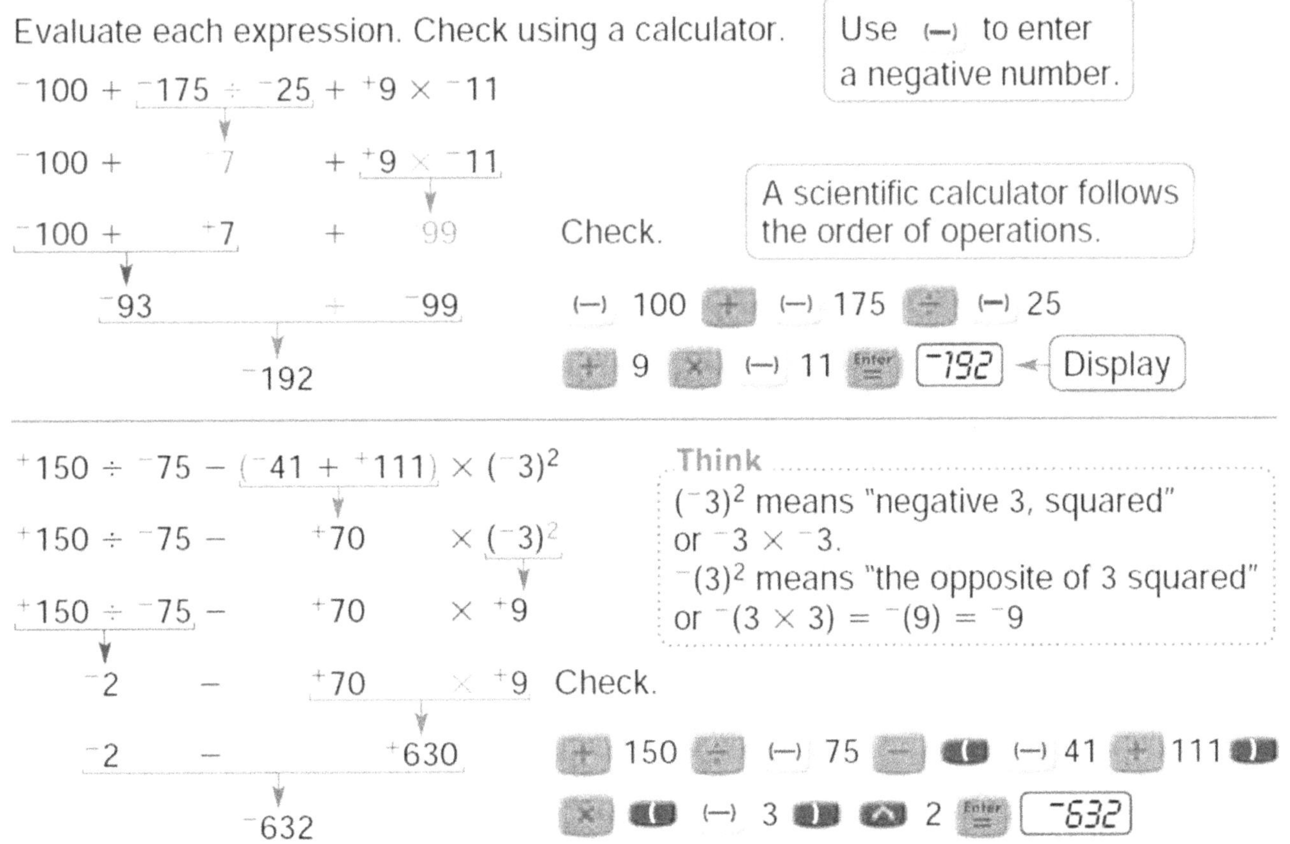

Complete the following operations…

1. $^-62 - {}^+84 \div {}^-4 + {}^+33$

2. $^-92 \times (^-91 + {}^+93) \div {}^-23$

3. $^+71 + {}^-175 - {}^+56 \div {}^-8$

4. $^+3 \times {}^-16 - (^+36)^2 \div {}^-12$

5. $^-4[6 + (8 - 5)^2]$

6. $^+4 \times [(^+6 - {}^-4)^2 \times 15] + {}^-5$

Compute. Watch the order of operations.

7. $^+16 - {}^-279 \div {}^+31$

8. $^-226 - {}^+190 \div {}^+10 + {}^-28$

9. $^+80 \div (^+93 + {}^-77) + {}^-304$

10. $^+67 + (^+68 - {}^+80)^2 \times {}^-30$

11. $7 - (^-9 - 5) \times 2^2$

12. $^-16 - {}^+4 \div (^+1 + {}^+1)^2$

13. $^-87 - {}^+60 \div {}^+15 + (^-40 + {}^+36)^2$

14. $^+24(^+45 + {}^-36) - {}^-21 - {}^+38 \times {}^+3$

15. $(^-24 \div {}^-3)(^-20 \div {}^+4) \div {}^+2$

16. $^-16 - {}^-14 + {}^-14 - {}^-16 + {}^-8 + {}^+3$

17. Three times of a natural number is subtracted from greatest number of three digits and the result is increased by 4,059 to get a value which is the desired result. Prepare a mathematical statement to solve this problem and find the value.

18. Mr. Torres spent \$85.50 for tickets to the National Aquarium for his family. The tickets cost \$19.50 for each adult and \$13.50 for each child. If three adults went to the aquarium, how many children went?

19. Mohanlal can finish half of a work in 7 days while working 8 hours a day. Sohanlal can finish quarter of the same work in 4 days while working 7 hours a day. Both of them started working jointly 7 hours a day to finish two such project works in ……. days.

20. Sum total of 7th multiple of 700, 8th multiple of 800, 9th multiple of 900, 5th multiple of 5,000 and 3rd multiple of 3,030 is increased by adding six digit smallest number. Prepare an order of operation to solve this problem. Also find the final result.

21. Sum total of first 50 consecutive natural numbers is divided by 51 and the value is increased by adding 23rd multiple of 2,002. Find the result.

22. $[2 \times (1 + 2 + 3 + \ldots\ldots + 100) \div \left(1 + \frac{1}{100}\right) \times 5,000 = \ldots\ldots\ldots\ldots$

23. Twentieth multiple of 2,020 + 30th multiple of 3,030 + 40th multiple of 5,050 = …. $\times$ 1,010.

H. O. T. S.

Sheet I

1. $12 + 7 \times 9^2$ **2.** $6 \times (7 - 4)^2 + 13$ **3.** $14 \times (6 + 79) \div 7$

4. $19^4 - 100 + (85 - 4 \times 2)$ **5.** $156 \div 3 \times 7^3 + 19$ **6.** $(19 \times 6)^4 + 214 \div 2$

Evaluate. Use a calculator to check your work.

7. $12 + 7 \times 9^2$ **8.** $6 \times (7 - 4)^3 + 13$ **9.** $10^4 \times (6 + 78) \div 7$

10. $19^2 - 100 + (85 - 4 \times 2)$ **11.** $156 \div 3 \times 7^2 + 19$ **12.** $(20 \times 6)^2 + 214 \div 2$

13. $(4 \times 7 + 5)^2 \div 11 + 1$ **14.** $87 - 54 + 12 \times 5^3$ **15.** $3^3 \times (15 + 19 - 10) \div 9$

16. $(9^2 - 19) + 42 \div 6 \times 2^3$ **17.** $51 + 5^2 \times 31 + 18^2 - 9 \times 7$

Compare. Write <, =, or >.

18. $16^2 \times 5 - 90 \ \underline{\ ?\ } \ 90 \times 5 - 16^2$ **19.** $(64 + 192) \div 8^2 \ \underline{\ ?\ } \ 64 + 192 \div 8^2$

20. $195 \div 5 \cdot 9^2 \ ? \ 195 \div (5 \cdot 9)^2$ **21.** $17(3)^2 \cdot (18 - 3) \ ? \ 17 \cdot 3^2 \cdot (18 - 3)$

22. Half of a square number exceeds three digit greatest number by 251. Find the number.

23. A train covers half of a km in 25 seconds. Length of this train is 600 m. Find out the time taken by this train to cross a telephone tower of negligible width.

24. Rikin can finish half of a project work in 8 days and Sikin can finish quarter of the same project work in 4 days. Both of them jointly can finish three such project works in ………….. days.

25. A solid cylinder has _____ flat faces and _____ curved faces.

26. The product of all the factors of 121 is ________ less than its greatest factor.

   A: 1   B: 11   C: 1,452   D: 1331

27: Two bells toll at an interval of 6 seconds and 8 seconds respectively. They toll together at 11:55 a.m. When do they toll together again for the second time?

Sheet II

Compute. Use a calculator to check your work.

1. $63 \div (2^2 + 3) - 7$ **2.** $21 + (0.8 + 6.4) \div 1.2$ **3.** $(3.2 + 4.3) \div 2.5 \times 3^3$

**Write as an expression, equation, or inequality.
Use a variable when necessary.**

4. Six less than a number is 3.   **5.** 25 more than 7 times a number

6. the sum of a number and 41.5   **7.** A number doubled is greater than 484.

8. Half of ten is three less than eight.   **9.** Forty is the product of x and five.

10. $5z$ decreased by 3   **11.** The sum of z and 35 is less than 98.

Evaluate each expression.

12. $(x + 2)^2 + y \div z$, when $x = 1$,   **13.** $r(q - 24) + w \div 2$, when $r = 3$,

14: Ruchika observed that a 300 m long goods train is taking 45 seconds to cross a light-post. Find the average speed of that train. Also find the time taken by that train to cross a 1500 m long railway platform.

15: Compare the place value of 5 in 235,934 and 54,435. Find difference of both the place values.

16: The shopping mall sells 148.14 liters of apple juice on Tuesday and 14.81 liters more than this quantity on Wednesday. The following day, 28.09 liters less apple juice was sold than the quantity sold on Wednesday. How many liters of apple juice was sold on Thursday?

17: If ray OD is perpendicular to line AB, and $\angle DOC = 30°$, find the value of $\angle BOC - \angle AOC$.

18. Two diagonals of a parallelogram AC and BD intersect each other at O. $\angle AOD = 70^0$. Find magnitude of rest of the other three angles formed at point o.

19: The sum of the digits of two-digit number is 10, while when the digits are reversed, the number decrease by 54. Find fifth multiple of that number.

20. What least number must be added to six digit smallest multiple of 9 to make the value a common multiple of 2, 4, 6 and 12?

21. Is there any pair of number having HCF 121 and LCM 1,690?

Sheet III

Choose the greater integer. Use a number line to help.

1. $^+7, ^+10$ **2.** $^-9, ^-3$ **3.** $^+3, ^-5$ **4.** $^-7, ^+6$

5. $0, ^-9$ **6.** $^+8, 0$ **7.** $^-12, ^-25$ **8.** $^+20, ^-20$

Compare. Write <, =, or >.

9. $^-10$ _?_ $^+6$ **10.** $^+4$ _?_ $^+8$ **11.** 3 _?_ $^-6$ **12.** $^-3$ _?_ $^+4$

13. $^+7$ _?_ 0 **14.** $^-4$ _?_ $^+4$ **15.** 0 _?_ $^-3$ **16.** $^-2$ _?_ $^-5$

17. $|^-8|$ _?_ $|^+7|$ **18.** 0 _?_ $^-|8|$ **19.** $|^-6|$ _?_ $^-(6)$ **20.** $^-(^-7)$ _?_ $^-(^+4)$

21. $^-|11|$ _?_ $^-13$ **22.** $^-(^+13)$ _?_ 0 **23.** $|^+12|$ _?_ $|^-12|$ **24.** $^-(^-10)$ _?_ $^-|^-20|$

Arrange in order from least to greatest.

25. $^+6, ^+8, ^+7$ **26.** $^-10, ^-8, ^-6$ **27.** $^-6, 0, ^-3$

28. $^+9, 0, ^+3$ **29.** $^-5, ^-6, ^-3, ^-7$ **30.** $^+4, ^-2, ^+5, ^-4$

31: Somanthika worked for 8 hours a day to finish half of a project work in 14 days. She wanted to work for 7 hours a day to finish the same project work in ………. days.

32. Write T for true and F for false:
    p. Two lines are parallel if they do not meet at any point, even when produced.
    q. Two lines are perpendicular to each other if they make a right angle at their point of intersection.

Aid Box: …

Write each repeated addition as a multiplication sentence.

1. $^+9 + ^+9 + ^+9 + ^+9 + ^+9 + ^+9$ **2.** $^-6 + ^-6 + ^-6 + ^-6 + ^-6 + ^-6$

3. $^+12 + ^+12 + ^+12 + ^+12 + ^+12$ **4.** $^-15 + ^-15 + ^-15 + ^-15$

Write the sign of the underlined factor for the given product.

5. $^-5 \times \underline{9} = ^+45$ **6.** $^+8 \times \underline{12} = ^-96$ **7.** $^-9 \times \underline{15} = ^-135$

8. $\underline{11} \times ^+12 = ^+132$ **9.** $\underline{7} \times ^-26 = ^+182$ **10.** $\underline{17} \times ^-22 = ^-374$

Find the product.

11. $^-75 \times 0$ **12.** $25 \times ^-13$ **13.** $0 \times ^+21$ **14.** $^-15 \times ^-12$

15. $^-7 \times ^-9 \times ^-4$ **16.** $5 \times ^-8 \times ^-12$ **17.** $(4 + ^-2) \times 6$ **18.** $8 \times |^-9 + ^-2|$

Sheet IV

Write an addition sentence that is modeled by each number line.

1. 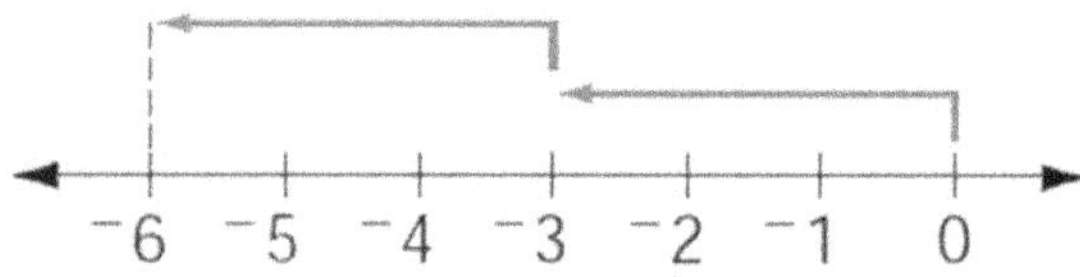

2. 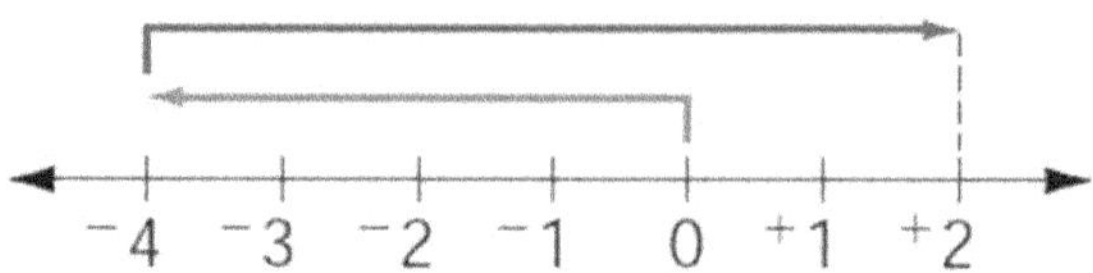

Add. Use a number line to help.

3. $^+2 + {}^+1$

4. $^-4 + {}^-3$

5. $^-1 + {}^-4$

6. $^+6 + {}^+1$

7. $^-6 + {}^+4$

8. $^+7 + {}^-5$

9. $^-5 + {}^-6$

10. $^+4 + {}^+4$

11. $^-4 + {}^+8$

12. $^-8 + {}^+5$

13. $^+6 + 0$

14. $0 + {}^-8$

15. $^+4 + {}^-5 + {}^-6$

16. $^-6 + {}^-2 + {}^+4$

17. $^-3 + {}^-3 + {}^-3$

18. $^-2 + {}^-2 + {}^-2$

19. $^+7 + {}^-5 + {}^-2$

20. $^-8 + {}^+6 + {}^+9$

21. Sum total of 100 consecutive natural numbers is equal to 5,050. Find product of second and greatest number of that number series.

Aid Box …. Divide and write the result.

1. $^+54 \div {}^-6$

2. $^-25 \div {}^+5$

3. $^-80 \div {}^+10$

4. $0 \div {}^+9$

5. $^-10 \div 0$

6. $^+11 \div {}^-1$

7. $^-20 \div {}^+1$

8. $^-4 \div {}^-4$

9. $\dfrac{^-36}{^-6}$

10. $\dfrac{^-1}{^+1}$

11. $\dfrac{50}{^-10}$

12. $\dfrac{^-80}{5}$

Divide to complete each chart. Then write the rule.

13.

IN	OUT
$^+8$	$^-4$
$^+10$	$^-5$
$^+12$	$^-6$
$^+14$	?
$^+16$	?
?	$^-9$

14.

IN	OUT
$^-30$	$^+5$
$^-24$	$^+4$
$^-18$	$^+3$
$^-12$	?
$^-6$	?
?	0

15.

IN	OUT
$^-24$	$^-3$
$^-16$	$^-2$
$^-8$	?
0	?
?	$^+1$
$^+16$	$^+2$

Sheet V

1: Which of the following pairs of angles are complementary?

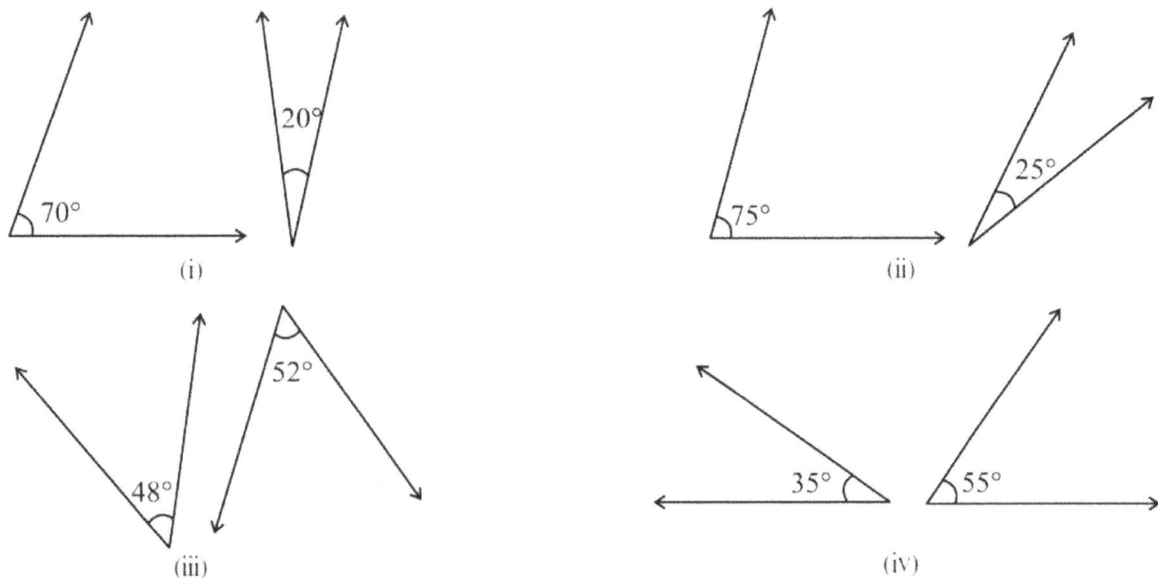

2: Observe the give pairs of angles and find out the statement which is not correct.

A: All the four options of angles are supplementary pairs.

B: Sum of angles of each pair is equal to a straight angle.

C: All the paired angles as displayed in four combinations cannot form straight angles.

D: Paired angles can form a linear pair if they share one of the arm and vertex in common.

3: Find out supplementary angle of complementary angle of 23^0.

4: Four angles of an irregular quadrilateral are in the ratio of 2: 3: 4: 6. Find magnitude of each of the angles of the quadrilateral.

5: Find pairs of supplementary angles.

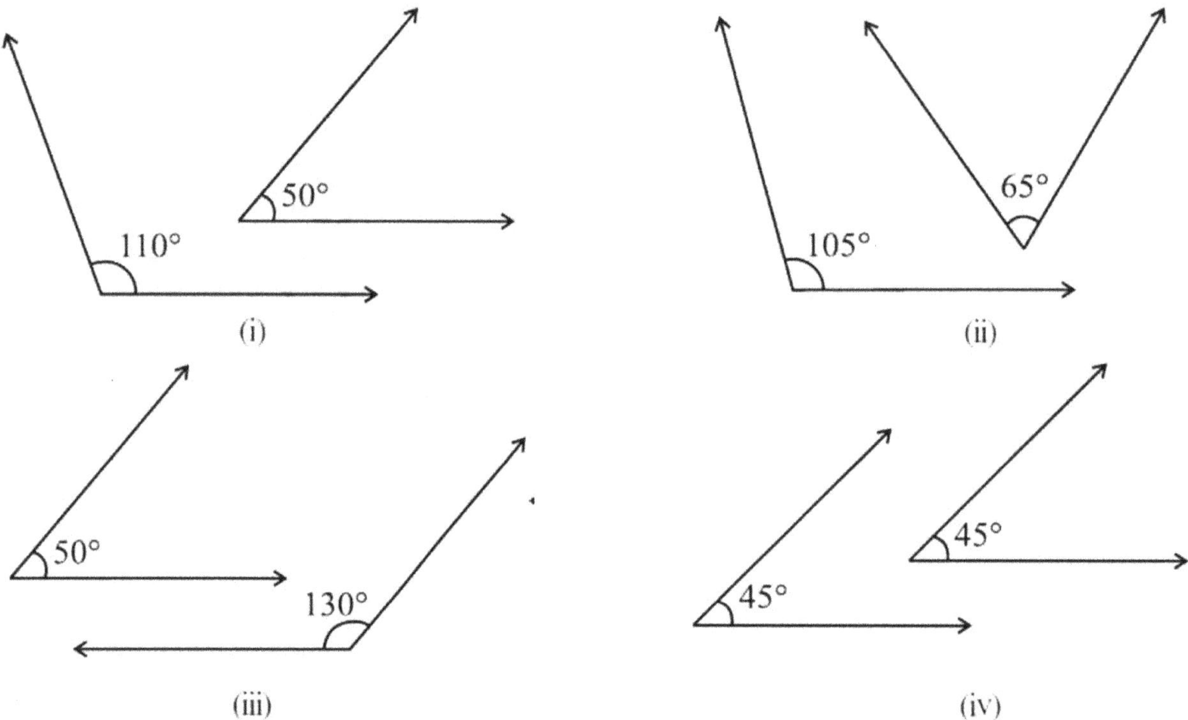

6: Find Complement and supplement

a. Find the complement of each of the following angles:

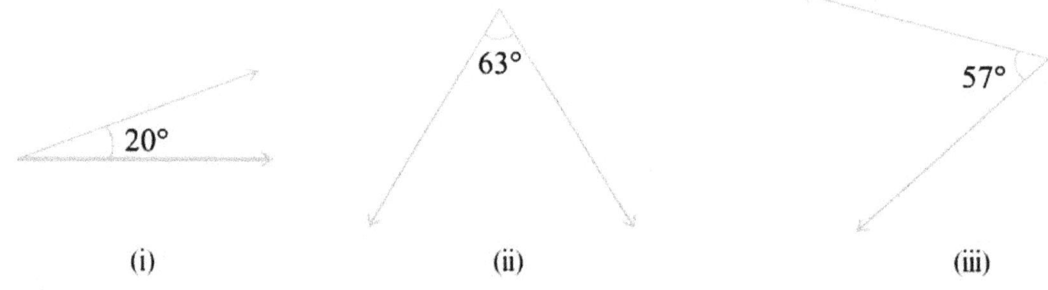

b. Find the supplement of each of the following angles:

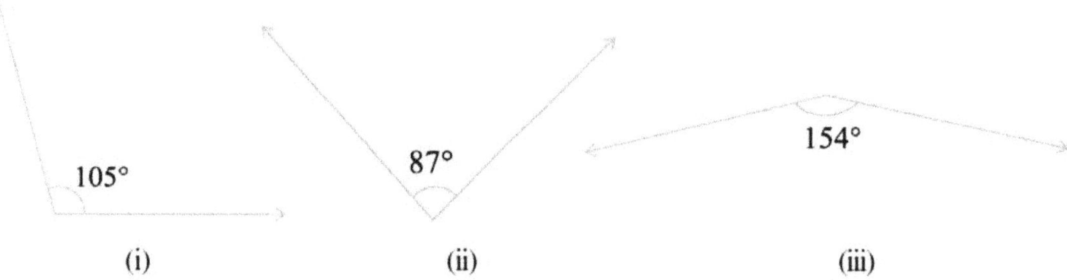

7: Three angles of a triangle are in the ratio of 1: 2: 3. Find each of the angles.

Combined Worksheets

WS I

Move decimal points.

$$
\begin{array}{r} 2\ 8\ 1 \\ \hline 2.3\,)\,6.4\ 6\ 3 \end{array}
$$

1. 2.3)6.4 6 3 **2.** 0.1 9)0.1 7 4 8 **3.** 0.9 2)2.8 6 1 2

1. quotient 2 8 1

2. quotient 0 9 2

3. quotient 3 1 1

4. 0.8)4.8 2 4 — quotient 6 0 3

5. 0.0 1 1)0.0 9 3 5 — quotient 8 5

6. 0.0 1 2)0.0 0 1 4 4 — quotient 0 1 2

7. 1.5)0.0 0 4 5 — quotient 0 0 0 3

8. 0.1 8)0.0 3 6 — quotient 0 2

9. 0.0 2 4)0.0 0 1 4 4 — quotient 0 0 6

Divide and check.

10. 0.5)7.55 **11.** 0.6)9.66 **12.** 0.4)0.76 **13.** 0.7)8.61

14. 92.4 ÷ 0.4 **15.** 6.3 ÷ 0.3 **16.** 257.2 ÷ 0.4 **17.** 0.96 ÷ 0.8

18. 2.214 ÷ 0.9 **19.** 0.084 ÷ 0.3 **20.** 555.6 ÷ 0.6 **21.** 391.2 ÷ 0.4

22. There were 6416 trees in a forest. In another forest there are three eighth more trees than the first one. Trees in a third forest is equal to 550 less than those of all the trees of both the first and second forest put together. Arrange these forests in accord to the increasing number of trees.

23. Find the perimeter of a figure formed by joining three equilateral triangles of side 23.23 cm each.

24 . Nithin is 40 m South West of Kavita. Mohini is 430 m South East of Kavita. Mohini is in which direction of Nithin ?

25 . Add: $16\dfrac{9}{10} + 106\dfrac{19}{100} + 21\dfrac{3}{1000} =$

26 . Veena rides her bike to the park for 18 minutes at an average speed of 9 m per second to meet a friend. Veena arrives at the park at 11:00 a.m. and stays there for 58 minutes. Her friend will arrive there at 12:15 p.m. they had a meeting for 32 minutes.

    Try to answer the following questions.
    A. What is the distance between the park and Veena's house?
    B. How long could Veena have to wait for her friend?
    C. How long does Veena stay at the park?
    D. When will Veena leave to go home?

WS II

Divide. Round to the nearest tenth.

1. $6\overline{)8}$ 2. $17\overline{)6}$ 3. $9.2\overline{)20}$ 4. $6.5\overline{)15}$

5. $2.3\overline{)0.4}$ 6. $0.9\overline{)2.1}$ 7. $3.1\overline{)6.5}$ 8. $0.3\overline{)0.8}$

9. $0.4\overline{)0.85}$ 10. $0.4\overline{)1.23}$ 11. $0.03\overline{)0.11}$ 12. $0.09\overline{)0.61}$

Divide. Round to the nearest hundredth or nearest cent.

13. $6\overline{)5}$ 14. $3\overline{)22}$ 15. $7\overline{)9.2}$ 16. $4\overline{)1.5}$

17. $1.1\overline{)4.5}$ 18. $1.5\overline{)0.4}$ 19. $3.3\overline{)8.1}$ 20. $0.7\overline{)4.5}$

21. $0.06\overline{)7.1}$ 22. $0.07\overline{)9.3}$ 23. $0.7\overline{)0.58}$ 24. $0.3\overline{)0.71}$

25. $8\overline{)\$1.24}$ 26. $6\overline{)\$8.23}$ 27. $2\overline{)\$1.11}$ 28. $3\overline{)\$5.19}$

29. Arrange the following shapes as per their increasing number of faces.

Cylinder, Sphere, Cuboid, Triangular Prism, Rectangular Pyramid.

30. A train is running at an average speed of 80 km per hour. It is covering up 4 km 4 m more in every interval of 10 minutes than that of a car. Find the average speed of the car.

31. A half filled oil container is used to store residue oil of capacity 125 liters. After filling the residue three eighth of the container remained empty. Find the capacity of the container.

32. One tenth of a container is equal to 16 cans of capacity 8 liters each. The entire container can hold ___________ liters of oil.

33: What least number must be subtracted from 219.376 to make the result exactly divisible by 219?   [Ans: 0.157]

34: A train, moving at the speed of 15 m per second, is taking 20 seconds to cross a telephone post. This train can take _______ seconds to cross a 1.5 km long platform. [Ans : 2 minutes]

35: Roshanlal can finish a work in 16 days while working 5 hours a day. He can finish the same work in ……….. days while working 4 hours a day.

WS III

Estimate each quotient. Use compatible numbers.

1. $3041 \div 82$ **2.** $300{,}864 \div 66$ **3.** $736 \div 4.2$ **4.** $37.26 \div 7.1$

Write in scientific notation.

5. 0.000056 **6.** 0.00158 **7.** 0.00012 **8.** 0.00000235

Find the quotient.

9. $0.83 \div 1000$ **10.** $9\overline{)189{,}567}$ **11.** $4\overline{)\$14.24}$ **12.** $0.7\overline{)7.91}$

13. $0.558 \div 6.2$ **14.** $0.032\overline{)0.288}$ **15.** $4.26\overline{)17{,}615.1}$ **16.** $0.25\overline{)7.625}$

Write each mathematical expression as a word phrase.

17. $98m$ **18.** $62.5 \div q$ **19.** $45 \cdot 25$

Find the value of each algebraic expression for $c = 0.3$ and $d = 2340$.

20. $d \div 6 \times 30$ **21.** $c \times d \div 1000$ **22.** $36 \div c \times d$

23. Write a number greater than 1, 50,000 by using digits 5, 4 and 2.

24. 324 thousands = ___________________ tens.   **25.** 32 crore = ___________ thousands.

26. ___________ crore is 400 greater than 99,99,600.

27. Write a number smaller than 39 lakhs by using digits 4, 3 and 8. Digits can be repeated.

28. Write the predecessor of 7 digit greatest even number.

29. Calculate the sum total of place values of 3 in the following numbers

       34,55,67,505,   30,56,05,506 and 35,05,04,050

30. Difference of the place value and face value of 8 in 65,76,80,653, 78,806 and 48,65,678 =

________________.

31. Numbers divisible by 2 are also called ___________ numbers.

32. All prime numbers have only _______ factors. _____ and the number itself.

33. Sum total of 2 eve numbers is always an _________ number.

34. A prime number between 95 and 100 = ___________.

35. All the multiples of 8 are also multiples of 2 and _______.

36. All the multiples of _____ and 4 may or may not be a multiple of 8.

37. All the multiples of ____ and _____ are not necessarily multiples of 10.

38. All multiples of 10 are also multiples of _______ and _______.

WS IV

Tell which operation is to be done first. Then compute.

1. $3 \times 9 + 8$

2. $16 \div 4 + 2$

3. $15 - 6 \div 3$

4. $\dfrac{7 + 11}{9} \times 3$

5. $21 - \dfrac{9 + 11}{10}$

6. $27 \div \dfrac{9 \times 3}{5 + 4}$

7. $(14 \div 2) + 6^2$

8. $2^2 \times [15 - 3]$

9. $64 \div (8 \times 8)$

Use the order of operations to compute. Justify each step in the process.

10. $4 \times 8 \times 3 - 2$

11. $18 \div 6 \div 3 - 1$

12. $9 + 3 \times 2 + 4^2$

13. $12 - 3 \times 1 + 2^3$

14. $(40 \div 4) + 5 - 3 + [0.6 \times 40]$

15. $5 + (34 - 2) \div 8 + (1.7 + 2)$

16. $10 \times 3 + (48 \div 6)^2 \times 0.4$

17. $(50 \div 10)^3 \times 2 + 6 \times 0.6$

18. $\dfrac{7 + 3}{2^2 + 1} - [5 \div 5 \times 2]$

19. $(24 + \dfrac{1 \times 7}{3^2 - 2^3} - 6) \div 5^2$

20. Rani is buying light bulbs for her Christmas decorations. She buys 1020 but when she gets to the cash, she has to put back 3 hundred 13 because they are broken. How many light bulbs does Marie buy?

21. There are two combinations of packs containing pens and pencils. Packet one containing 6 pens and 5 pencils costs Rs 128. Packet B containing 5 pens and 6 pencils costs Rs 103. Calculate the cost of a new pack containing 10 pens and 10 pencils of such type?

      A: Rs. 250   B: Rs. 120   C: Rs. 135   D: Rs. 210

22. Difference of digits of a two digit number is 7. If digits are reversed then sum total of both the number becomes the predecessor of the three digit smallest number. Find the second multiple of this number.

23. Temperature of a city increased by $8\,^0$ C last week. If a corresponding increase of temperature in ^{0} F is 1.8 times more than that of the value in ^{0} C , then find the value of such increase of temperature in ^{0} F

***.

Model Papers

Model Paper I

1. Kavita had a piece of rope of length 9.5 m. She needed some small pieces of rope of length 1.9 m each. How many pieces of the required length will she get out of this rope?

2. In a survey of 22,000 people, 14,300 responded that watching T.V. was the most important consideration in their daily life. What percent of the people felt that watching T.V. was not the most important consideration?

3. Three boys earned a total of Rs 64.54 less than Rs. 300. What was the average amount earned per boy?

4. 45% of a number is 10 less than a hundred. Find the number.

5. Ravi earned $ 90 in a week. Calculate his annual income.

6. Interior angles of a triangle are in the ratio of 1:2:3. Find all the angles.

7. What least number must be added to the 7 digit greatest number to make it divisible by 11?

8. A shopkeeper issued three consecutive discounts of 10% on certain purchase. Find the single equivalent discount.

9. This number is the reciprocal of itself. It is also the only factor of itself. Find the number.

10. Find a natural number which is also a multiplicative inverse of 0.125.

11. 7 tenths is _______________ more than 17 hundredths.

12. One third of a number exceeds the three digit greatest number by 18. Find one fourth of that number.

13. Selling Price of 6 apples is equal to Cost Price of 8 apples. Find the gain percentage.

14. What least number must be added to the sex digit greatest number to make it divisible by 8?

15. Cost of a pen and a pencil is $ 6. Cost of 3 pens and 5 pencils is $ 22. Find the cost of 5 pens and 7 pencils. Also find the cost of a pencil.

16. Reshma uses ¾ m of cloth to stitch a shirt. How many shirts can she make with 12 m cloth?

17. Complete the following:

    a. A number that consists of a whole number and a fraction is called a/an ______________?

    b. 2. An______________________ is a number that represents a part of a whole.

    c. 3. A fraction whose numerical (absolute) value is greater than 1 is called a/an __________________,

    d. and a fraction whose numerical value is between 0 and 1 is called a/an ________________

    e. 4. ________________ mean the same value.

18. Pallavi attended a birthday party at 9:35 P.M. She stayed there for 1 and half hours. By what time she will be returning back?

19. Ten metal cubes of volume 10 cu.cm each melted and casted again to form a larger cube of edge ________ cm.

20. Two sides of a triangle are 6 cm and 13 cm. The length of the third side must be in between ______ cm and ____ cm.

21. ______ % of 15 = 0.75

22. ____ % of 10 % of 150 = Half of 0.3

Model Paper II

1. Any Principal amounts to double with 12% rate of simple interest in _________ years.

2. Reflex angle of quarter of a right angle is _______ less than a complete angle.

3. Mohan increased the price of a product by ______ % to receive 10% profit instead of a 10% loss.

4. Three identical cubes of edges 15 cm each joined side by side to make a cuboid. Find the sum total of both base and top surface of that cuboid.

5. $\frac{1}{11} X \frac{121}{139} X \frac{278}{144} X \frac{12}{101} X \frac{505}{123} =$ _________

6. Ratio of the supplementary and complementary angles of certain angle is 2:7. Find the angle.

7. Particle A covers 32 m in 8 seconds. Particle B covers 60 km in 1 hour. Which particle is moving faster and by how much?

8. Score of Neeta was 15 less than her 90 % score in the session end exam. There were 5 subjects of 100 marks each. Find her score.

9. The product of two proper fractions is _________ than each of the fractions that are multiplied.

10. While dividing a fraction by another fraction, we __________ the first fraction by the _________ of the other fraction.

11. What least number must be subtracted from a six digit greatest number to make it a multiple of 4?

12. Find a greatest number that can divide 129, 654 and 504 leaving remainder 4 in each case.

13. Complete the following:

    a. The reciprocal of a _________ fraction is an improper fraction.

    b. The reciprocal of an improper fraction is a _________ fraction.

    c. Product of two fractions =

    Product of their ____________ / Product of their __________

    d. The product of two ___________ fractions is less than both the fractions.

    e. A _____________ of a fraction is obtained by inverting it upside down.

    f. To multiply a decimal number by _________, we move the decimal point in the number to the right by three places.

    g. To divide a decimal number by _________, we move the decimal point in the number to the left by two places.

    h. ______ is the only number which is its own reciprocal.

14. What percentage of all the numbers starting from 1 to 100 are multiples of 12?

15. $(1 + 2 + .. + 20) = (1 + 20) \times 20/2 = $ .... In the same way calculate the following:

$(1 + 2 + 3 + ... 100) - (1 + 2 + .. + 50) = $ ....

16. Rithika can finish a project activity in 20 days. Her friend Sunitha can finish the same project in 10 days. Both the friends joined hands to finish the project before time. Find the total time taken by them to finish the project activity.

17. Total number of diagonals in a pentagon is ....

18. How many right angles will be equal to sum total of all the exterior angles of a pentagon?

19. What least number should be subtracted from a 6 digit common multiple of 5 and 10 to obtain a common multiple of 3, 6 and 9?

Model Paper III

1. 13 dam = _______ dm.

2. What happens to the value of a fraction if the denominator of the fraction is decreased while numerator is kept unchanged?

3. Which letter comes $2/5^{th}$ of the way among A and J?

4. In a class of 40 students, $1/5^{th}$ of the total number of students like to eat rice only, $2/5^{th}$ of the total number of students like to eat bread only and the remaining students like to eat both. What fraction of the total number of students likes to eat both?

5. Niharika read $1/5^{th}$ pages of a book. If she reads further 40 pages, she would have read 710th pages of the book. How many pages are left to be read?

6. How many 1/16 kg boxes of chocolates can be made with 1.5 kg chocolates?

7. For the sale of every 10 mangoes a shopkeeper gains the cost price equal to a mango. Find his gain percentage.

8. $\left(1 - \frac{1}{2}\right) X \left(1 - \frac{1}{3}\right) X \left(1 - \frac{1}{4}\right) X \ldots \left(1 - \frac{1}{100}\right) = 0.\underline{\quad}$

9. 10 workers can finish a work in 36 days. _______ more workers required to finish the same job in 6 days.

10. Length of a diagonal of a square of side 25 cm is __________ cm.

11. Ratio of three angles of a triangle is 2:3:4 . Find all the angles.

12. The mean of three consecutive numbers is 42. Find the numbers.

13. Calculate the difference of area and outer boundary of the following triangle. Another triangle of the same dimension is fitted below it. What type of figure of what dimension will be obtained? What will be the perimeter of that figure?

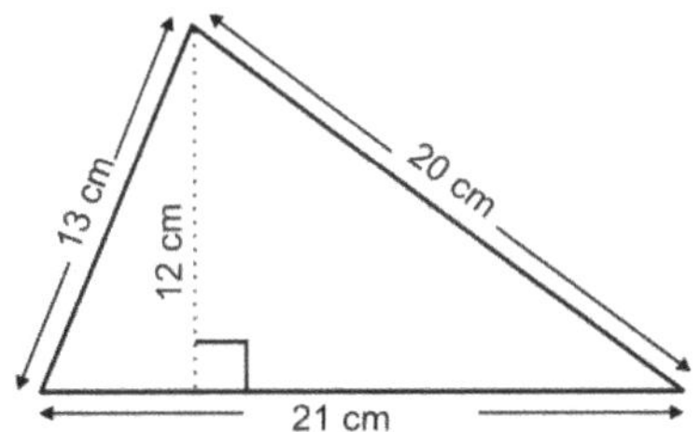

20. What least number must be added to 100 to make it divisible by 11?

Model Paper IV

1. $3333 X 3333 \div 9999 =$ ___

2. Nikita is 21 years younger than her aunt. Her aunt will be 3 times her age after 4 years. Find the age of Nikita.

3. For preparing 16 gift packs containing 4 pencils, 12 sketch pens and 4 pens club members used 144 pens. Calculate the numbers of sketch pens and pencils used by them. Also find the numbers of packets duly prepared.

4. $ 27,000 is divided amongst three friends at a ratio of 11:9:7. Find the share of all the three friends.

5. Sum total of two numbers is 7 and their difference is 2. Find the sum total of the reciprocals of both the numbers.

6. What least number must be added to a seven digit smallest odd number to make it a multiple of 9?

7. 12% of 21% of 10,000 = ___ .

8. Dr Sarkar reached his chamber 5 minutes late, but the wall mount clock was displaying a time to show that he has reached his chamber 12 minutes before. The wall mount clock of the chamber is running fast by _____ minutes. Actual time when Dr Sarkar reached his chamber was __________.

9. Find the value of $\frac{(1+n)}{n^2}$

$$\left(1 - \frac{9}{10}\right) X \left(1 - \frac{99}{100}\right) X \left(1 - \frac{999}{1000}\right)$$

9. Find the value of x.

$$\cfrac{8x}{1 + \cfrac{1}{1 + \cfrac{x}{1-x}}}$$

10. 72519 X 9999 = _______ .

11 . 7/8th of 24,000 books were distributed to three public libraries in the ratio of 11:6:4. Find the number of books received by all the three libraries.

12 . Namitha in 16th from the front and 23rd from the back side of a row. How many students are there in that row?

13.
$$\left(1 - \frac{1}{10 + \frac{1}{10}}\right) + \frac{11}{19} + 17\frac{7}{38} + 23\frac{3}{38}$$

14. Sum total of digits of a two digit number is 9. If 27 added to it its digits are reversed. Find the number.

15. $2[\left(1 - \frac{1}{10}\right)\left(1 - \frac{1}{11}\right)\dots\left(1 - \frac{1}{1000}\right)] = ?$

16 . A plant grows at a rate of certain fixed rate per week and attained a height of 208 cm in a year. Finds its regular rate of growth.

17 . A shopkeeper increased the price for certain item by 20% and issued a discount of 20%. Find the total profit or loss percentage on his overall transactions.

18 . Two objects at average speed of 60 km/h and 72 km/h are moving in a same direction. The gap between them at initial was 72 km. The faster object was following the slower one. It will cross the slower object after ____ hours and gain an advantage of 224 km after ____ hours.

19. By what rate percentage per annum simple interest certain sum becomes 8/7th of the principal in 5 years?

20 . If 15% 0f a = 17% of b then find the value of $(a + b)^2 - (a - b)^2$

20 . Nitin gained 10% by selling a bat to Harish. Harish again sold it to Munish at a gain of 8%. If Munish paid Rs 654 for the bat, find its original price.

21 . PQRS is a rectangle. E and G are mid points of PQ and RS respectively. Both the diagonals bisect each other at point F. The ratio of total area of triangle PFQ and triangle EFR to that of the total area of the rectangle is ___________.

22. How many percentage of numbers in between 1 and 77 are square numbers?

23: Sides of an isosceles triangle are in the ratio of 5:5:6. Height of this triangle from its base to vertex angle is 16 cm. Find its perimeter.

24: A batsmen's average before the last two innings of a season was 66. He failed to score in those innings and his average dropped to 55. How many innings did he play that season.

Aid Box: Representation of Fractions…

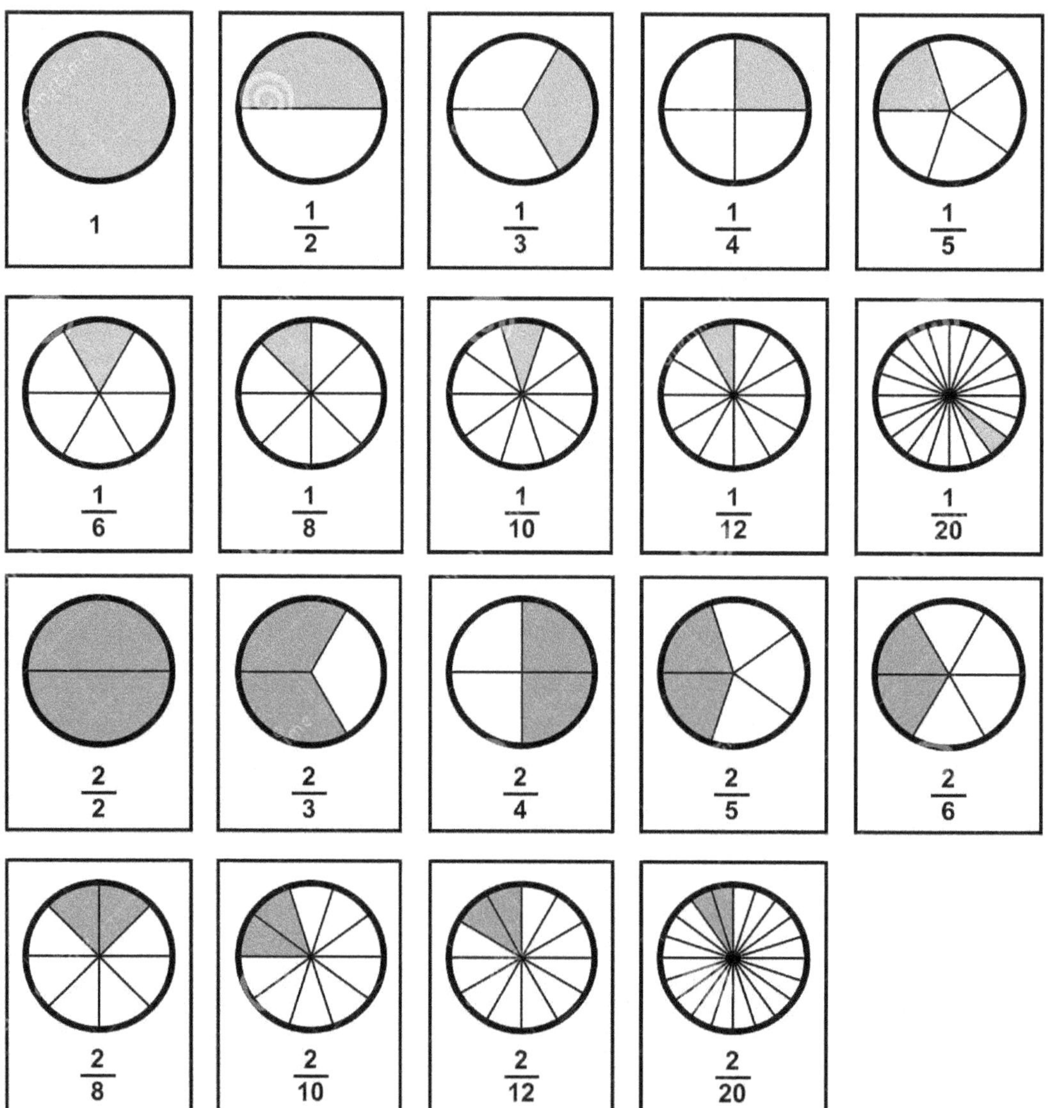

Model Paper V

1. Temperature of a city increased by $5\ ^0$ C last week. If a corresponding increase of temperature in ^{0} F is 1.8 times more than that of the value in ^{0} C , then find the value of such increase of temperature in ^{0} F

    A: 18^0 F　　　B: 9^0 F　　　C: 8.9^0 F　　　D: $6\ ^0$ F

2. A racing car covers 100 km in 2 hours and another 400 km 4 hours. The speed of the car during second time is _____ times more than that of the first time.

    A: 1　　　B: 2　　　C: 3　　　D: 4

3. The product of the place values of 5 in the following number is _________

    32,435

    A: 9,000　　　B: 90,000　　　C: 9,00,000　　　D: 900

4. What must be added to 10932 to make it exactly divisible by 9?

5. $$\frac{3}{6},\ \frac{7}{6},\ \frac{1}{6},\ \frac{5}{6},\ \frac{11}{6}$$

    If we arrange these fractions in ascending order, then denominator of the product of 2nd and 3rd fraction in simplest form will be ____________

    A: 12　　　B: 24　　　C: 36　　　D: 48

6. Half of one sixth of 72 is the _________ multiple of three.

7. A wire of a square sized shape of side 32 cm is reshaped to form a circle. Find the circumference of that circle. [Circumference of a circle is the outer boundary of a circle].

8. A solid cylinder has _____ flat faces and _____ curved faces.

9. The product of all the factors of 121 is _________ less than its greatest factor.

    A: 1　　　B: 11　　　C: 1,452　　　D: 1331

10. Two bells toll at an interval of 6 seconds and 8 seconds respectively. They toll together at 11:55 a.m. When do they toll together again for the second time?

    A:　12:19 pm

    B: 12:19 am

    C: 12: 24 pm

11. Ruchika observed that a 300 m long goods train is taking 45 seconds to cross a light-post. Find the average speed of that train. Also find the time taken by that train to cross a 1500 m long railway platform.

12. Compare the place value of 5 in 235,934 and 54,435. Find difference of both the place values.

13. A milk-dairy produces 25,545 liters of milk every day. It supplies 15,625 liters of milk to a milk-depot and the rest to the market. How much milk is supplied to the market?

14. The sum of two numbers is 94506. One of the numbers is 49605. Find the other number.

15. The sum of two numbers is 45650. One of the numbers is 22587. Find the other number. Which part of the sum is the given number?

16. There are 35,278 students in Class III, 32,184 students in Class IV and 25,375 students in Class V in the schools of a city. Find the total number of students reading in Classes III, IV and V. Among these students 60,324 are girls. Find the number of students who are boys.

17. A person had $ 197,865. He gave $ 50,753 to his wife and $ 75,928 to his son. The rest of the money he gave to his daughter. How much did the daughter get?

18. What should be added to the sum of 3,46,068 and 3,24,263 to get the sum of 8,05,400?

19. Sum total of a number and its reciprocal is 8.125. Find the product of that number and the respective reciprocal.

20. There are 4021 students in a school. Each section can accommodate a maximum number of 25 students. There are equal number of students in each section, find their number in each section. Is there any section having less than 25 students? How many such sections are there?

21. Write in standard form:

32 tens + 54 hundreds + 121

= ___________ .

Model Paper VI

1. Find the digit present in the thousands place in the product
2. $(11011 \div 11) \times 7{,}000 =$ ______________
3. $(121 \div 11) \times 8{,}000 =$ ______________
4. $(12310 \div 11) \times 9{,}000 =$ ______________
5. $(12221 \div 121) \times 6{,}000 =$ ______________
6. Sum total of the smallest and the greatest four digit numbers formed by without repeating any digits twice is ______________ more than the smallest five digit number.
7. 432 hundreds + 232 tens + 32 ones = ______________________ .
8. $9{,}876 + 1{,}023 =$ ______________.

9. Difference of digits of a two digit number is 7. if digits are reversed then sum total of both the number becomes the predecessor of the three digit smallest number. Find the second multiple of this number.
10. Compare the place value of 3 in 2,309 and 3,283. Find the difference of both the place values of 3. The difference is the _(____) th multiple of 100.
11. 121, 169 and 219 have following things in common:
    I. All these numbers are square numbers.
    II. These are square numbers of odd primes.
    III. These numbers have equal numbers of   prime factors.
    Select which of the statements mentioned above are true.
    A: Only I   B: Only II
    C: Both I and III   D: All
12. Complete the Prime factorisation:
    a) 141   = ____ X____;
    b) 84 = __________________;
    c) 363 = ________ X ________ ;
    d) 3,000 = 2 X 2 X 2 X ________
    e) 729 = _ X __X___ X ___X__;
    f) __________ = 89 X 11

13. In the calculation table depicted below numbers are related to each other. Find their inter relations and also identify missing numbers.
14. 32 X 10,000
    = ______ X 16 = ______ X 8.

15. 8th multiple of 16 is ________________ multiple of 32.
16. 9th multiple of 11 is ________ multiple of 9.
17. After subtracting ____________ we can obtain 3rd multiple of 13 from the 4th multiple of 10.
18. Complete the following:
a) 1, 4, 9, ___i___, ___ii___, _iii_;

b) i X ii + iii = _________________

c) 1, 8, 27, ____, ___ __ , __   _ .

d) 121, ___, _____ , _______ 161.

e) 64, ____, ___ , _______ , 16, 9.

19. Product of all the factors of 6 = _________

A: 36   B: 12

C: 18   D: 24

20. How many diagonals are there in a pentagon?

21. Rohan added 2001 to a number instead of subtracting 201 from that number. Find the difference of his actual and desired result.

22. What least number should be added to the seven digit smallest number to make it a dividend of 11 and 2?

23. Some of the statements regarding prime and composite numbers are given below.

I : 1 is not a prime *or* composite number.

II : Two is the only even prime number.

III: All odd numbers are not prime.

IV: All composite numbers can be written as product of prime numbers.

V: 101 has only two factors 1 and the number itself. That is why it is a prime number

Which of the above statements are true?

A: Only I   B: All

C: I, II and III

D: II, III and IV

Model Paper VII

1. A teacher purchased three types of pens. 6 boxes of red pens with 40 pens in each box. 5 boxes of blue pens with 20 pens in each box. Which number is closest to the total pens?

   A: 250　　　B: 350　　　C: 400　　　D: 450

2. All the three digit numbers formed by using digits 4, 3 and 0. If you arrange these numbers in ascending orders then _______a_______ comes in the second position and ___b___ comes at last.

   Find the value of (3a + 4b)(3a – 4b)

3. Mr Jordon prepares to put fencing around his rectangular kitchen garden of width 95 m and the length 105 m. How long fencing wires does he need?

   A: 190 m　　B: 200 m

   C: 210 m　　D: 400 m

4. Half of the half of 98 = ___________ of 196.

5. Sum total of all the numbers formed by using digits 1,3 and 0 only once is ___________.

6. _______ is the only number which is a factor of all the numbers.

7. ________ is the predecessor of smallest six digit odd number.

8. Find the digit present in the thousands place in the product

   (11011 ÷ 11) X 7000 = ______

   A: 1　　　　B: 11　　　　　C: 121　　　D: 111

9. $\frac{1}{72}$ of a circle is equivalent to ___________

   A: 72^0　　　B: 36^0　　　　C: 5^0　　　D: 10^0

10. $\frac{1}{72}$ + $\frac{1}{72}$ + $\frac{1}{72}$ + $\frac{1}{72}$ = $\frac{...}{36}$

    A: 1　B: 2　C: 3　D: 4

11. Mandela wanted to add three digit greatest number to another number to obtain a five digit smallest number. He has added ___________ to the third multiple of 333.

12. _____________ is the predecessor of 4 digit greatest even number.

13. At 1 O Clock and 11 O Click both hour hand and minute hand of a clock makes an angle of ___a______ which is __b__ of a complete angle.

         A: a= 90^0 b = $1/4^{th}$ B: a= 180^0 b = $1/2^{nd}$

         C: a= 270^0 b = $1/3^{rd}$ D: a= 30^0 b = $1/12^{th}$

14. At 3 O Clock and 9 O Click both hour hand and minute hand of a clock makes an angle of ___a______ which is __b__ of a complete angle.

A: a= 90^0 b = $1/4^{th}$

B: a= 180^0 b = $1/2^{nd}$

C: a= 270^0 b = $1/3^{rd}$

D: a= 30^0 b = $1/12^{th}$

15. One fourth of a scale is equal to one tenth of another scale. For measuring a ribbon of 8m the longer scale is used ten times. Find the length of the shorter scale.

     A: 1 m   B: 2 m   C: 3 m   D: 4 m

16. Compare the place value of 3 in 2,309 and 3,283. Find the difference of both the place values of 3. The difference is the _(____) th multiple of 100.

     A: 27   B: 30   C: 28   D: 35

17.. _______ is the difference between 4th multiple of 9 and 6th multiple of 100.

      A: 636   B: 536   C: 564   D: 546

18. __________ is the only even prime number.

19. 2, 3, ______ and ______ are first four prime numbers.

20. Add: 100 + 3 tens + 32 hundreds + 12 ones = __.

Model Paper VIII

1. A chimp is taking a multiple-choice test. Of course the chimp can't read and is guessing for every question. If there are 4 choices for each question, and there are 84 questions on the test, how many questions can we expect the chimp to answer correctly?
   (hint: There is a 25% chance that the chimp will guess correctly.)

2. First tap can fill a water tank in 30 minutes and second tap can empty the half filled tank in 1.5 hours. By what time the empty tank will be filled up if both the tap kept open?

3. After increasing the selling price of an item by 10% the profit percent on that item is increased from 12% to 15%. Find the ratio of Cost Price and Selling Price of that item.

4. A merchant paid $500 for a table. He then marked it $820. If he then allowed the buyer a 25% discount, how much was the selling price?

5. A sofa cost a merchant $500. He priced the sofa so that he could allow a customer a 25% reduction from the marked price and still make a 23% profit.

6. Certain bank offers a deposit scheme at a simple rate of interest under which any principal doubles itself in ten years of time. Find the rate of interest.

7. If $\frac{1}{x} = \frac{1}{y} = \frac{1}{z} = \sqrt[3]{81}$, $p = \frac{xy+yz+zx}{xyz}$, then $p^3 - 1 =$ _.

8. Half of a cake is given to all friends, half of the remaining portion of the cake retained by parents, one third of what remaining was distributed amongst John's classmates. Finally John received only 200 g of the cake. Find the quantity of that cake.

9. Complete the number series:

   a. 1.1.2.3.5._____,____, ______.

   b. $\frac{1}{3}, \frac{3}{5}, \frac{5}{.7}, \ldots \ldots \ldots$ Ratio of 10th and 15th value = _________.

   c. $1, 8, 27,$ _____ , $a, b, \; c \ldots$; here a, b and c are 5th , 6th and 7th member of the series. Find $\frac{(b-c)}{a}$.

10. Population of a city increased by 10% consecutively two times in two successive years. An equivalent single increase of population by percentage = _______ %.

11. 15% of a population completed their service life. 32% of the rest of population are going to complete their service life this year. Rest of the others remains employed during the next year. Find the ratio of employed and retired person during next year.

12. Josephine is on an 1,800 calorie per day diet. She tries to keep her intake of fat to no more than 30% of her total calories. Based on an 1,800 calorie a day diet, what is the maximum number of calories that Josephine should consume from fats per day to stay within her goal?

13. Solve the following equation:

$$x : y : z = 1 : 2 : 3;$$

$$a = \frac{(xy + yz + zx)}{xyz} \; ;$$

$$a^2 + 2a + 3 = \underline{}$$

14. Arrange in ascending order:

$$\sqrt{0.81}, \; \sqrt[2]{0.0121}, \quad \sqrt[3]{0.0625}, \; 25^{-\frac{1}{2}} , \; 125^{-\frac{1}{3}}$$

15. A can of mixed nuts contains 80% peanuts. If the can holds 16 ounces, how many ounces of peanuts does it contain?

16. If a % of b is equal to 0.09, then find the value of $\frac{a^2-b^2}{ab}$.

17. A state sales tax rate is 12%. If the tax on a purchase was $24, what was the price of the purchase?

18. 10% of 10% 0f 10% of a number = a% of that number. Find the value of a.

19. 25 is what percentage of 625 ?

20. One third of a = three fourth of b. Which value is bigger and by how much?

21. There was a consecutive increase of medicines by 10%, 12% and 15% . Find a single equivalent percentage increase of the product.

22. If $p = \frac{(8.5^4 - 1.5^4)}{8.5^2 - 1.5^2}$, then find the

value of $\frac{p+1}{p-1}$.

23. What least number must be added to a six digit greatest number to make it divisible by 4?

24. If a$=\left(1 - \frac{1}{100}\right) .... \left(1 - \frac{1}{1000}\right)\left(\frac{100^2-1}{101}\right)$,

then find the value of $\left(\frac{a^2+a+1}{a^2-a+1}\right)\left(\frac{a-1}{a+1}\right)$.

25. If 10% of a = 15% of b = 20% of c,

then a: b: c = ______________.

Model Paper IX

1. P = 515.15 −15.51−1.51−5.11− 1.11.
   Find the value of 2P + 1

2. If a = (7.5 × 7.5 + 37.5 + 2.5 × 2.5), then find the value of
$$\frac{a^2+1}{a^2-1} - \frac{a^2-1}{a^2+1}$$

3. A began a business with Rs 45000 and B joined after wards with Rs 30000. At the end of a year, the profit is divided in the ratio 2:1. When did B join ?

4. An employer reduces the number of his employees in the ratio 7: 5 and increases their wages in the ratio 15 : 28. State whether his bill of total wages increase or decrease and in what ratio.

5. In three vessels, the ratio of water and milk is 6 : 7, 5 : 9 and 8 : 7 respectively. If the mixtures of the three vessels are mixed together, then what will be the ratio of water and milk ?

6. A drum contains 20 liters of a paint. From this, 2 liters of paint is taken out and replaced by 2 liters of oil. Again 2 liters of this mixture is taken out and replaced by 2 liters of oil. If this operation is performed once again, then what would be the final ratio of paint and oil in the drum ?

7. If a : (b + c) = 1 : 3 and c : (a + b) = 5 : 7, then b : (a + c) = ___.

8. 15 men, 18 women and 12 boys working together earned Rs 2070. If the daily wages of a man, a woman and a boy are in the ratio 4 : 3 : 2, the daily wages (in Rs) of 1 man, 2 women and 3 boys are _______________.

9. Ratio of the incomes of A, B and C last year was 3 : 4 : 5. The ratio of their individual incomes during the last year and this year are 4 : 5, 2 : 3 and 3 : 4 respectively. If the sum of their present incomes is Rs 78800, then find the present individual income of A, B and C.

10. 10% of A = 20% of B = 30% of C. Find the value $\dfrac{AB+BC+AC}{ABC}$.

11. $\dfrac{1}{10}$ of a number x exceeds $\dfrac{1}{15}$ of another number y by 5. Find the value of P.

$$P = \dfrac{3x-2y}{3x+2y} + \dfrac{3x+2y}{3x-2y}.$$

12. Tap A can fill a tank in 30 minutes and tap B can fill the same tank in 40 minutes. Both the tap can fill the tank jointly in _____ mins.

13. In two alloys, copper and zinc are related in the ratio of 4 : 1 and 1 : 3. 10 kg of 1st alloy, 16 kg of 2nd alloy and some of pure copper are melted together. An alloy was obtained in which the ratio of copper to zinc was 3 : 2. Find the weight of the new alloy ?

14. Railway fares of 1st, 2nd and 3rd classes between two stations were in the ratio 8 : 6 : 3. The fares of 1st and 2nd class were subsequently reduced by $\dfrac{1}{6}$ and $\dfrac{1}{12}$ respectively. If during a year, the ratio between the passengers of 1st, 2nd and 3rd classes was 9 : 12 : 26 and the total amount collected by the sale of tickets was Rs 1088, the collection from the passengers of 1st class was _____________.

15. Salary of Mark is increased by 16%. His previous salary was _____ % less than that of the increased salary.

16. Solve the following equation :

$$\dfrac{11}{144} \ X \ \dfrac{12}{169} \ X \ \dfrac{13}{121} \ X \ \dfrac{132}{341} \ X \ \dfrac{682}{1001} \ X \ \dfrac{13}{19} =$$

17. What least number must added to the smallest six digit number and must be subtracted from the largest five digit number to make both of them a multiple of 11?

Model Paper X

1. 1. Calculate Simple Interest paid by a bank on Rs. 3,000 for 5 years at the rate of 8% per annum.

2. Bank A pays a Simple Interest Rs 200 on a deposit of Rs 20,000 in 1 year. Bank B pays a Simple Interest Rs 300 on a deposit of Rs. 30, 000 in 2 years. Which bank is paying more rate of interest?

3. Half of a cake is 125 g more than 3/4th of a bread. Find the total mass of 2 cakes and 5 breads.

4. Rohini wanted to paint 2/3rd of a rope, 1/3rd of the rest of the rope blue and the terminal part of the remaining rope green. Find the percentage of such rope which is painted green.

5. In an assignment 45 mathematical problems were given to all the students. Bandana can solve 30 mathematical problems in an hour. Her brother Rachit can solve 4/5th of all problems in 40 minutes. Rohini can solve 8/9th of these assignments in 50 minutes. Arrange these students in accord to their speed of calculations.

6. Bhavini covered 8/15th of the entire track of a race in 80 minutes. She has another 1.5 km to go. Find the additional time that she need to finish her race without changing her speed. Also find her speed.

7. Marina added 20% of 120 and 40 % of 140 to obtain a number. If 30% of 30 is added to it, it will become a prime number having only two factors, 1 and the number itself. Find out that prime number.

8. Rohini prepared a cup of 200 ml, which can hold water equal to 1/11th of a bowl, 1/25th of a can and 1/100th of a bucket. Calculate the total capacity of all the containers.

9. The difference of the length of the geometry box and scale of Andrea is 6.2 cm. sum total of both the length is 30 cm. find the length of both the object.

10. Mohan and Ravi prepared a Robotic toy which can cover a distance of 173 cm in 20 stepping. Calculate the distance covered by that robot in 180 stepping.

11. The predecessor of a five digit smallest number is the __________ digit greatest number.

12. Four electric lights are turned on at the same time. First one blinks every 4 seconds, second one blinks every 6 seconds, third one blinks every 8 seconds and the fourth one blinks every 12 seconds. In 60 seconds, how many times will they blink at the same time?

13. Every 2nd, 5th and 10th visitor of a shopping complex receives gifts. How often do three visitors at a time will receive gifts?

14. Before last Saturday there was a rain. Weather station speculated advent of another rain after a couple of fortnight. Which of the forthcoming day would be a rainy day?

15. A circular ring was reshaped to design a square of side 39 cm. what was the circumference of the ring?

Model Paper XI

1. What least number must be subtracted from a three digit greatest number to make it a common multiple of 2, 4 and 8?

2. Find the arithmetic mean of 21, 32 , -74 and 1029.

3. Find the arithmetic mean of first 100 natural numbers.

4. Arithmetic mean of three consecutive odd numbers is 27. Find all the three odd numbers.

5. Submit your answer

6. The average of 199 numbers is 1050. From these numbers average of first 99 members is 900. Find the average of the remaining numbers.

7. A 132 m long train takes 20 seconds to cross a light post. Find its average speed in km/h. If the same train moves continuously for 45 minutes then the distance covered by it will be …………. Km.

8. 8. Fractions like ½, 1/3, ¼, 1/8, 1/12, are also called ______________ fractions.

9. 9. Difference between 0.005 and 0.05 = ______

10. 1232.4054 =

11. 1043,546 =

12. $\dfrac{21}{100} + \dfrac{132}{1000} + \dfrac{4321}{10000} =$ ______________

13. $\dfrac{11}{144} \; X \; \dfrac{12}{121} X \dfrac{11}{139} \; X \; \dfrac{13}{125} X \dfrac{12}{25} =$

14. 10,000 + 32 hundreds + 29 tens = ____________.

15. An ice cream truck began its daily route with 95 gallons of ice cream. The truck driver sold 78% of the ice cream. How many gallons of ice cream were sold?

16. In a survey of 22,000 people, 14,300 responded that salary was the most important consideration in their ideal career. What percent of the people felt that salary was not the most important consideration?

17. Forty-nine percent of all people who buy running shoes don't run at all. Assuming 340,000 people buy running shoes, how many will use them to run in?

18. In a month Mark makes a 22% down payment on a home in Mumbai . What was the purchase price of the home if her down payment is Rs. 35,200?

19. A family wants to keep the expenditure on sugar intact in the condition of a 20% increase in the cost of sugar. The family will curtail the consumption of sugar by _____ % for doing the same.

20. What percent of hour is equal to 76 seconds?

21. Niharika wanted to give half of a quarter of Choco bar to her friend and half of the remaining Choco bar to her younger sister. Her younger sister will receive _____% of the entire Choco bar.

22. Angles having a common arm and a common vertex are called adjacent angles.

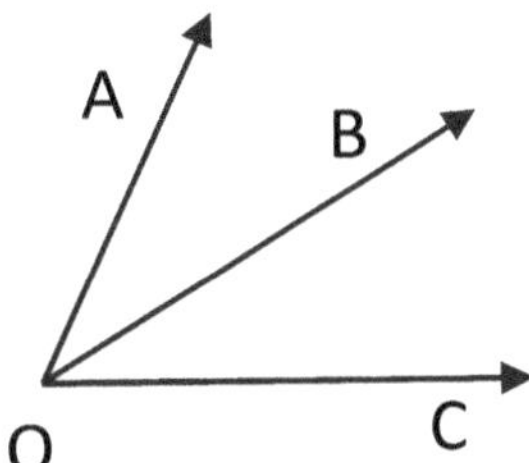

In the given figure ___________ and ___________ are adjacent angles sharing a common arm OB.

23. Find the area enclosed by the sector AOB in the given circle having radius 21 cm.

24. Find the ratio of circumference and area of the circle.

25. What percent of circle is the sector AOB?

26. Compare areas of two circles of 21 cm and 28 cm respectively.

27. Two concentric circles of radius 28 cm and 35 cm will enclose a ring like area of _______ sq. cm.

28. _________ non overlapping triangles can be fitted inside a hexagon.

29. How is 106.076 written in word form?

____

30. 17. Write 16 tenths and 16 thousandths in standard form?

____

Model Paper XII

1. Which fraction of the given figure is shaded?

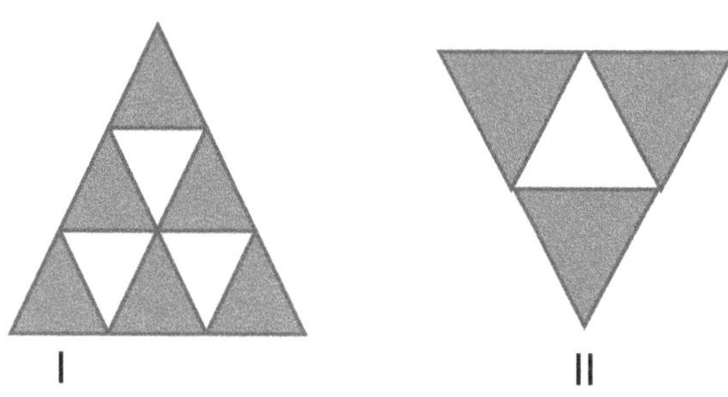

2. Points located on same line are called _______________ points.
3. A line has no _________________ but a line segment has ___ such ______ ____________.
4. A ________ can be extended endlessly in any one direction.
5. A ______ can be extended endlessly in both the directions.
6. 32 hundreds + 32 hundredths = _____________.
7. Instead of writing 321 thousands Rita has written 3 lakhs 12 thousands. Find the difference between the original and the derived answer.
8. Which natural number is having only one factor?
9. 21 tenths = _______________ hundredths.
10. Half of a gross = _________ dozens.
11. Total cost of 5 pens and 6 pencils is Rs. 145. Total cost of 6 pens and 5 pencils is Rs. 251. Find individual cost of a pen and a pencil. Also find the total cost of 5 pens and 3 pencils.
12. List all the factors of 16. Find the sum total of all these factors.
13. 5 km 5 m = _________________ m
14. Sam has a collection of 963 comic books. What are the five different ways Sam could divide his comic books into equal groups?
15. Sum total of all the factors of 6 = _________. This sum total is _____ times greater than the number itself.
16. A study table is 2 m long and 1.5 m wide. Another large table is thrice as long and twice as wide as the study table. What is the area of both the table?
17. Cost of fencing a square shaped garden at the rate of Rs. 120.00 per m was Rs. 48,000.00. Find the length of a side of that garden.
18. At the end of the party, the kids broke open the gift packs. When they assembled all the candy, Bill got 9 pieces. Sara got 3 times as many pieces as Bill. Nitin got one third of the number of candies gathered by Bill. Which of the statements depicted below are true?
    I.   They have collected total number of candies which is also equal to third multiple of 3.
    II.   Sara got 4 times more than Nitin.
    III.   Share of Nitin and Bill was 15 less than that of Sara.
    IV.   Sara got 9 times more candy than that of Nitin.

19. A wall mount clock takes 2 seconds to toll 2 bells at 2 a.m. Find the time by that clock to toll 11 bells at 11 a.m.
20. What least number must be subtracted from 129.013 to make it a multiple of 129?
21. Which value can repeat itself even after multiplying it by itself?
22. Romanika counted a bundle of sheets, excluding that of top 15 ones, as 132. She has placed 21 sheets in to the printer. How many sheets were there in all?
23. Monika calculated 15th multiple of 5 added to 5th multiple of 15. Find the digit that she might have in the one's place of the product.
24. Complete the following …

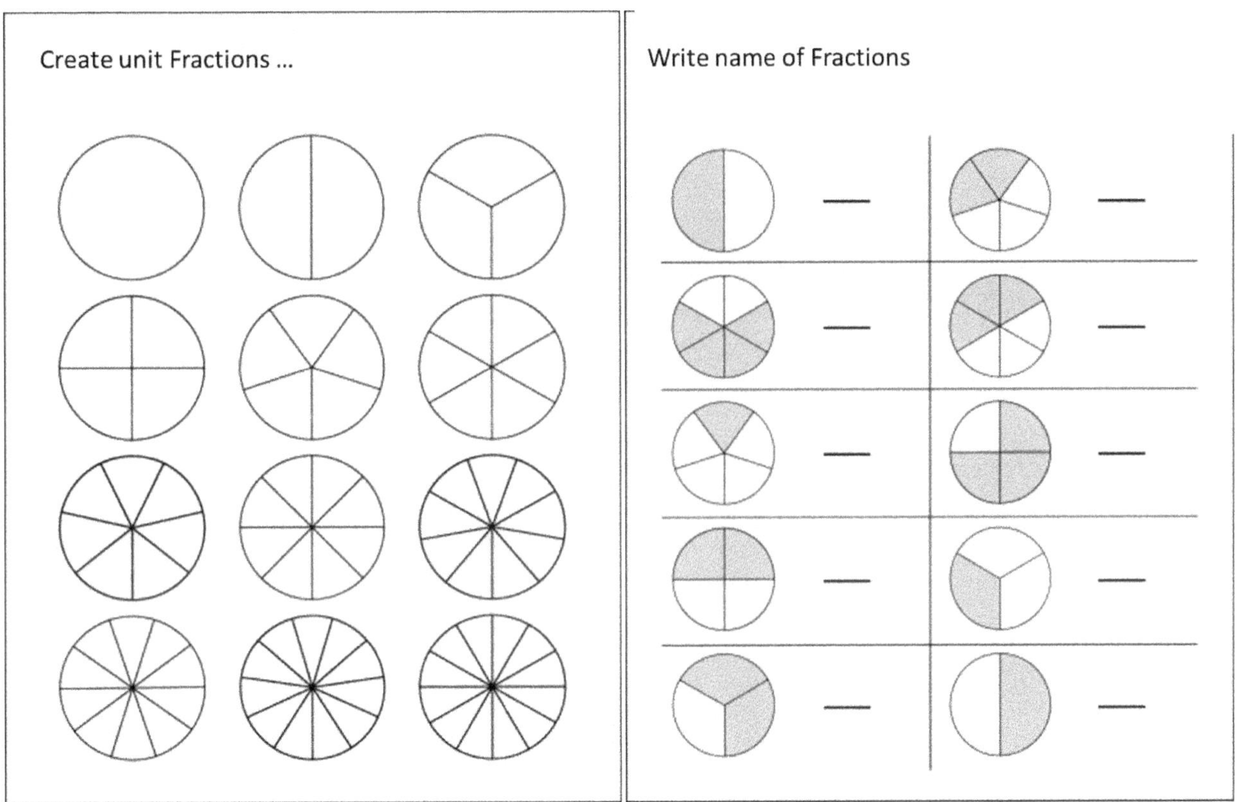

Model Paper XIII

1. What least number can be subtracted from the greatest number of five digits to make the number a multiple of 8?

2: There are _______ diagonals in a quadrilateral and ____ diagonals in a pentagon.

3: The smallest possible number which can be divided by 4, 8, 12 and 16 leaving a remainder 3 in each case will be __________.

4: Find the digit present in the thousands place in the product

a. $(11011 \div 11) \, X \, 0.7 \qquad = P;$
b. $(29029 \div 1001) \, X \, 0.11 \quad = Q;$
c. $(1010101 \div 101) \, X \, 0.005 = R;$
d. $(3090 \div 103) \, X \, 0.08 \qquad = S;$

P = 700.7   Q = 3.29   R =   50.005   S= 2.4

Statements:

I. They have values up to thousandths place in their like decimal from.
II. If arranged in ascending order, then Q comes at last.
III. All the results of P, Q, R and S are in decimal form.
IV. Sum total of the greatest and the smallest value is equal to a number which is 3.1 more than the seventh multiple of three digit smallest number.

Which of the above statements are not correct?

Options:

A: Only I, III and IV   B: Only II, III and IV

C: Only II   D: Only IV

5: After adding 0.125 to a decimal number the sum total becomes a decimal number having a position in the middle of 14 and 17. Find the place of that original number on the number

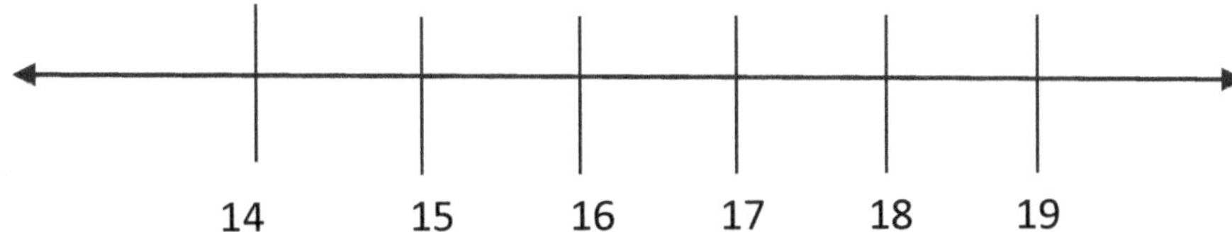

line provided.

6: What must be subtracted from the thousands place and tens place of the following number to make it a multiple of 9?

168,213

Options: _____ from thousandths place and ___ from tenths place.

Statements:

I.   There are more than two options possible for solving the same problem.

II.   Sum total of both the numbers to be subtracted respectively from thousands place and thousandths place will be always same.

III.   We must go for adding all the digits of the number before verifying it by using divisibility rule.

IV.   This problem can be solved without doing the actual division.

Which of the following statements are true?

A: Only II and IV   B: Only I and III   C: Only III   D: All

Model Paper XIV

Tell which numbers are divisible by 2.

1. 24   **2.** 6135   **3.** 47   **4.** 9842   **5.** 98   **6.** 7764
7. 436   **8.** 57,961   **9.** 569   **10.** 79,778   **11.** 760   **12.** 490,893

Tell which numbers are divisible by 5. Tell which are divisible by 10

13. 65   **14.** 35,960   **15.** 90   **16.** 45,782   **17.** 873

18. 73,590   **19.** 745   **22.** 94,615   **17.** 4000   **23.** 870,520
20. 9154   **21.** 791,621

Tell which numbers are divisible by 4.

25. 96   **26.** 82   **27.** 324   **28.** 422   **29.** 3820   **30.** 9416

31. 79,131   **32.** 83,536   **33.** 20,904   **34.** 72,072   **35.** 131,616   **36.** 806,300

Tell which numbers are divisible by 3. Tell which numbers are divisible by 9.

37. 69   **38.** 87   **39.** 135   **40.** 159   **41.** 4320   **42.** 3519

43. 71,415   **44.** 83,721   **45.** 95,580   **46.** 81,693   **47.** 100,512   **48.** 560,373

Tell which numbers are divisible by 6.

49. 84   **50.** 93   **51.** 204   **52.** 396   **53.** 1029   **54.** 5415

55. 11,712   **56.** 30,609   **57.** 28,514   **58.** 72,144   **59.** 503,640   **60.** 712,820

Write whether each number is divisible by 2, 3, 4, 5, 6, 9, and/or 10.

61. 1425   **62.** 2360   **63.** 4390   **64.** 6570   **65.** 8735   **66.** 9822

67. 12,360   **68.** 19,585   **69.** 23,130   **70.** 335,412   **71.** 240,120   **72.** 350,262

73: Complete the following number series:

a. 1, 1, 2, 3, …., ….., ……., ……….., …………,

b. 11, 121, 1331, ……….., …………………;

c. 1, 8, 27, ………, …………….., If this series continues then find the value of 10th step.

d. ,,,, ; ,,,,,,,,,, ……….., ………………., ………………, …………, 49, 64, 81, …………….;

Model Paper XV

Find the quotients. Look for a pattern.

1. $9 \div 3$
    $90 \div 3$
    $900 \div 3$
    $9000 \div 3$
    $90,000 \div 3$

2. $48 \div 6$
    $480 \div 6$
    $4800 \div 6$
    $48,000 \div 6$
    $480,000 \div 6$

3. $30 \div 5$
    $300 \div 50$
    $3000 \div 50$
    $30,000 \div 50$
    $300,000 \div 50$

4. $12 \div 4$
    $120 \div 40$
    $1200 \div 40$
    $12,000 \div 40$
    $120,000 \div 40$

5. $45 \div 9$
    $450 \div 90$
    $4500 \div 900$
    $45,000 \div 9000$
    $450,000 \div 90,000$

6. $56 \div 7$
    $560 \div 70$
    $5600 \div 700$
    $56,000 \div 7000$
    $560,000 \div 70,000$

Divide. Write the basic fact you use.

7. $7\overline{)350}$

8. $9\overline{)720}$

9. $3\overline{)1800}$

10. $8\overline{)6400}$

11. $80\overline{)240}$

12. $60\overline{)420}$

13. $50\overline{)300}$

14. $30\overline{)120}$

15. $50\overline{)2000}$

16. $40\overline{)2800}$

17. $60\overline{)3600}$

18. $20\overline{)18,000}$

19. $40\overline{)16,000}$

20. $700\overline{)49,000}$

21. $800\overline{)480,000}$

22. $300\overline{)270,000}$

Complete the following:

23. $1/5^{th}$ of $4,004 = $ ......

24. $1/11^{th}$ of $33044 = $ ....

25. $1/13^{th}$ of $39065 = $ ....

26. $11/19^{th}$ of $57095 = $ ....

27. 5th multiple of 99 + 99th multiple of $1,000 = $ ....

Write the following in the form of fraction:

28. 0.011 29. 0.125 30. 0.625 31. 64/1000   32. 0.025 33. 1.25

34. 0.0125 35. 0.75 36. 0.0625 37. 11.011   38. 25.075 39. 0.005

40. 0.064 41. 12.072 42. 1.025 43. 2.02   44. 5.05 45. 0.055

Write the digit in the tens place.

46. 39   47. 247   48. 6531   49. 78,093 50. 189,704

Write the digit in the hundreds place.

51. 563   52. 849   53. 7442   54. 65,104 55. 282,312

Write the place of the underlined digit.

56. 94$\underline{7}$2 57. 8435 58. 6$\underline{7}$,892   59. $\underline{6}$0,948   60. $\underline{3}$49,925

61. 17,539 62. 417,058 63. 502,931   64. 896,127   65. 642,573

66. Find the least number which can be added to a six digit smallest number to make the value divisible by 9.

Model Paper XVI

Complete each division.

1.
```
      2 R  ?
41)8 6
  -? ?
     ?
```

2.
```
       2 ?
32)6 7 2
  -? ?
     ? ?
    -? ?
       ?
```

3.
```
          9
47)4 2 1 6
   4 2 3

   Try  ?
```

```
           ? ? R  ?
47)4 2 1 6
  -? ? ?
     ? ? ?
    -? ? ?
       ? ?
```

Divide and check.

4. 32)96

5. 22)88

6. 41)205

7. 17)153

8. 61)854

9. 43)688

10. 34)680

11. 27)621

12. 51)358

13. 65)201

14. 82)331

15. 46)283

16. 35)1019

17. 76)3733

18. 44)1456

19. 63)3792

20. 59)1193

21. 36)2884

22. 43)3886

23. 72)4332

24. 45)9542

25. 62)6905

26. 81)9729

27. 76)9884

28. If we start dividing 11077 by 11 then quotient will be ....

29. Add all the natural numbers starting from 1 to 1,000 and divide the result by 1,001.

30. Form the greatest and smallest number of four digits formed by using digits 4,3 ,0 and 9 only once. Also find their sum total.

31. What fraction of all the natural numbers from 1 to 40 are multiles of 5? Find their sum total.

32. $(1 + 2 + 3 \ldots\ldots + 2{,}000) - (1 + 2 + \ldots + 1800) = $ ....

33. A rectangular park of dimension 200 m X 10 m is divided into 20 equal parts for developing floral garden. Find the area of each such smaller parts.

34. $1/13^{th}$ of 39065 + $1/19^{th}$ of 57095 + $1/27^{th}$ of 54081 = ...

Model Paper XVII

Estimate the sum or difference by rounding.
Then compute and compare.

1. $9\frac{1}{3} + 2\frac{3}{8}$ 2. $8\frac{2}{3} + 3\frac{3}{4}$ 3. $14\frac{1}{3} + 12\frac{1}{2}$ 4. $16\frac{2}{7} + 13\frac{5}{9}$

5. $11\frac{3}{5} + 4\frac{7}{8}$ 6. $16\frac{1}{4} + 4\frac{3}{8}$ 7. $19\frac{2}{9} + 15\frac{3}{4}$ 8. $15\frac{1}{8} + 14\frac{8}{9}$

9. $7\frac{1}{5} + 3\frac{4}{9} + 5\frac{1}{3}$ 10. $4\frac{2}{11} + 7\frac{1}{8} + 9\frac{3}{10}$ 11. $8\frac{3}{5} + 9\frac{4}{7} + 3\frac{5}{6}$

12. $8\frac{7}{12} - 4\frac{3}{4}$ 13. $10\frac{1}{5} - 2\frac{3}{10}$ 14. $18\frac{2}{9} - 4\frac{1}{2}$ 15. $15\frac{2}{3} - 4\frac{7}{8}$

16. $6\frac{4}{7} - 2\frac{1}{3}$ 17. $5\frac{7}{10} - 2\frac{3}{5}$ 18. $9\frac{2}{3} - 2\frac{5}{6}$ 19. $8\frac{3}{4} - 3\frac{2}{7}$

Estimate the sum or difference. Use front-end estimation.

20. $12\frac{1}{8} + 3\frac{2}{3}$ 21. $9\frac{8}{11} + 7\frac{2}{9} + 6\frac{1}{10}$ 22. $9\frac{4}{5} + 8\frac{3}{4} + 4\frac{1}{3}$

23. $9\frac{5}{16} - 6\frac{1}{5}$ 24. $10\frac{3}{5} - 4\frac{2}{3}$ 25. $18\frac{7}{12} - 5\frac{2}{7}$ 26. $25\frac{1}{8} - 13\frac{11}{15}$

27. $\frac{1}{10} - \left(\frac{1}{100} - \frac{1}{1000}\right) - \frac{2}{1000} =$ ....

28. $\left(1 - \frac{1}{10}\right) X \left(1 - \frac{1}{11}\right) ... X \left(1 - \frac{1}{1000}\right) =$ ....

29. $\left(\frac{101}{1000} + \frac{11}{100} + \frac{121}{10000}\right) X 10000 =$ ... ...

30. 1/12th of 840084 + 1/13th of 910091 + 1/11th of 770077 = ...X 7,007;

31. $11\frac{1}{10} + 121\frac{11}{100} + 12321\frac{121}{1000} =$ ....

32. (1 + 2 + 3 + 4 .... + 1000) X $\frac{1}{1000} =$ ....

33. Fifth multiple of 2,002 divided by tenth multiple of 100 = ...

Model Paper XVIII

36. How many different possible solutions can satisfy the following equation?
$$(x^2 - 5x + 5)^{(x^2-12x+45)} = 1$$

37. A three digit number is such that the number N = 100a + 10b + c. Again the number is a product of two factors b and 10c + b. Find the number.

38. An integer is a palindrome when the same number is obtained when digits are reversed. 121,253, 132 etc. are all palindromes. Find a number in such that n^2 will be a palindrome with 6 digits.

39. Sum of the digits of a smallest possible number N is 18. Sum total of all the digits of 2N is 27. Find out the value of N.

40. What least number must be added to a six digit smallest number to make the number 1210214 divisible by 74.

41. Evaluate the following.
$$\left(\sqrt{2} + \sqrt{11} + \sqrt{13}\right)\left(\sqrt{2} + \sqrt{11} - \sqrt{13}\right)\left(\sqrt{2} - \sqrt{11} + \sqrt{13}\right)\left(-\sqrt{2} + \sqrt{11} - \sqrt{13}\right)$$

42. Each interior angles of a heptagon is obtuse. Angles are multiples of 9. Find the degrees of sums of the two largest angles.

43. A three digit number is multiplied by 3 and 1 added to it, then the result is a reverse of the original number. Find the original number.

[Hints: (100 a+ 10b + c)X3 +1 = 100c + 10b + a   100 a+ 10b + c = ?]

44. If $ab = a^b$ and $\dfrac{a}{b} = a^{3b}$, find b^{-a}

45. $0.33 < \dfrac{m}{n} < \dfrac{1}{3}$. Find the smallest possible value of n to satisfy the above mentioned relationship.

46. Find the smallest seven digit number which is divisible by 11. What are the two digits will be there in tens and ones place of that number?

47. Mark deposited $ 23,500 in his savings bank account which was offering 4% simple interest per year. Find the amount that Mark will obtain after a tenure of 4 years and 5 months.

48. -4.5 + 5.64 + _______ = 0. Make this equation true.

49. Solve the following
   a. $7 \text{ X } 20 - 2 \text{ X } 4 + 3^2 + 12 \div 4$

b. $\dfrac{\left(\sqrt[3]{0.125}+\sqrt[2]{.0064}\right)}{\sqrt[3]{1.331}-\sqrt[2]{0.0081}}$

c. If $x+\dfrac{1}{x}=9$ then find the value of $(2x-9)^2$

50. A shopkeeper purchased 16 dozen bananas at the rate of Rs 24 per dozen and found that 5% of his stock became non sellable. Rest of his stock was sold at the rate of Rs 30 per dozen. Find out the rate percent of his gain or loss incurred in this business.

51. Simplify the following: $7[120 - 2(4 + 3)^2 + 12] \div 2$

52. X = 0.3333... + 0.4444 + 0.9999.. Find the value of $\dfrac{x+1}{x-1} + \dfrac{x-1}{x+1}$

53. Shweta joined a Yoga Centre and her body weight was reduced from 76 kg to 65.6 kg. Find the percentage weight loss that she made during the tenure of her exercises.

54. Base of a triangle is reduced by 5% and its height is increased by 5%. Find the total percentage increase or decrease in the area of the triangle.

55. All the five sides of a regular pentagon is 12 cm each and apothem is 8 cm. find the area of this pentagon.

[Hints: The apothem of a regular polygon is a line segment from the center of the polygon perpendicular to a side.]

56. A _____________ angle is an angle with its vertex at the center of a circle whose sides are radii.

57. Calculate the total surface area of a cuboidal room of dimension 8mX6mX5m.

58. Arrange the following values in ascending and descending order:

59. What is the next number in the following sequence: 2, 4, 8, 16, _______, _______ ?

60. Write 3/7 and 5/9 in their corresponding decimal form. What are the common things in both the decimal form?

61. The cost of a camera is reduced by 10% to make it equivalent to another camera having a selling price calculated on the basis of 10% profit on the cost price of 21,850. Find the original cost price of the first camera.

62. 3% of 600 is __________ less than 5% of 500.

63. A college offers 25% of all seats of the Graduate programme to local candidates. Last year 125 local candidates got admission in that college. Find the total seat capacity available in that college for Graduate programmes.

64. A shopkeeper offers two discounts of value 5% and 8% on an item. Calculate the equivalent discount of two such consecutive discounts.

65. Population of a city increases at the rate of 10% of previous year's population. Calculate the population of a city in which population before two years was 125,000. Also calculate the population of that city after two year.

66. Parking lot of a school is represented by an expression: $\frac{3}{4}\left(2(2 + 4k) + 2\left(3 + \frac{5}{6} k\right)\right)$

Convert this expression in simplest form.

67. 30% of a number is equal to 40% of another number. Calculate the ratio of both the number.

68. P = $\sqrt{20} - \sqrt{20} + \sqrt{20} - \sqrt{20} \ldots \ldots \ldots \infty$. Find the value of $P^2 + 3P - 20$.

69. $\sqrt{15}$ = 3.88. Find the value of $\sqrt{\frac{5}{3}}$.

70. A person moved on towards countryside at 6 O'Clock. He travelled certain distance at an average speed of 4 km/h, and then another distance at 3 km/h and again a distance at an average speed of 6 km/h. After reaching he turned back and reached the place from where he had started. That time it was 12 noon in his wrist watch. Find the distance travelled by him. [Ans: 24 km]

71. A 500 m long train crosses a telephone post in 20 seconds. The same train crosses a platform in 90 seconds. Find the length of that platform.

[Ans: 1 km 750 m]

72. Two trains of length 200 m and 400 m respectively. They cross each other in 15 seconds while moving in opposite direction and 75 seconds while moving in the same direction. Find speed of both the train. [Ans: 24 m/sec. and 16m/sec]

73. Normally Nikita performs her morning walk at an average speed of 12 km/h. Today her speed was 5/6th of the average. Because of this reason she was late by 10 minutes. Find the normal time that she spends daily for morning walk.

[Ans: 50 minutes]

74. Speed of a train was reduced from 65 km/h to 50 km/h. Earlier this train was taking 1.5 hours to cover certain distance. Now it will take _________ minutes more to cover the same distance. [Ans : 27]

75. In a kilometer race A beats B by 100 meters, B beats C by 100 meters. A beats C by _____ meters.

[Ans : 190 meters]

76. A bus moves a distance without stoppage at an average speed of 420 km/h. With stoppages the same distance is covered by that bus at an average speed of 28 km/h. find the hourly stoppage time of that bus.

[Ans: 20 minutes]

77. A 300 m long car is running at an average speed of 90 km/h. another car of length 200 m is running in the same direction at an average speed of 60 km/h. Find the time taken by the first car to overtake the second one.

[Ans: 50 seconds]

78. Length of a train is half that of a km long bridge. A train clears this bridge in 2 minutes. Find the speed of that train.

[Ans: 45 km/h]

79. A train of length 110 m passes a man, who is walking against it at an average speed of 6 km/h, in 6 seconds. The speed of this train is _____________.

[Ans: 60 km/h]

80. A boat running upstream takes hours 48 minutes to cover certain distance. It takes 4 hours to cover the same distance running downstream. Find the ratio between the speed of the boat and speed of the stream. [Ans: 8:3]

81. What fraction of numbers in between 1 and 50 are prime numbers?

82. What least number must be added to 1029.1016 to make it exactly divisible by 1029?

83. Third multiple of a prime number which is greater than 90 and less than 100 = ______.

84. Complete the following:

    a. $a^3 b^4 c^5 \times a^3 b^7 = $ _____

    b. $a^5 b^8 c^5 \div a^3 b^7 = $ _____

    c. $\dfrac{1}{\dfrac{1-\dfrac{1}{1-x}}{x-1}} + \dfrac{1}{\dfrac{1-\dfrac{1}{x^2-1}}{x+1}} = $ __________.

    d. $\left(1 - \dfrac{9}{10}\right)\left(1 - \dfrac{99}{100}\right)\left(1 - \dfrac{999}{1000}\right) = 10 - - - -$

85. Find the value of $\dfrac{m^2+1}{m^2-1} - \dfrac{m^2-1}{m^2+1}$,   if $\sqrt[3]{m} = \left(1 - \dfrac{1}{2}\right)\left(1 - \dfrac{1}{3}\right) \dots \left(1 - \dfrac{1}{1000}\right)$

86. If $\dfrac{2}{1 + \dfrac{1}{1 + \dfrac{x}{1-x}}} = 1$,   then find the value   of $\left(\dfrac{x+1}{x-1}\right)^2 + \left(\dfrac{x-1}{x+1}\right)^2$.

87. Reciprocal of $x^8 = $ ____________.

88.

Model Paper XIX

1. Find the value of x if $x^2 + x + 1 = 0$.

2. Capacity of three cans is in the ratio of 1:2:3. Smallest can holds 200 ml less than a liter of any liquid. Find capacity of all the cans.

3. Find the two largest numbers of four digits having 531 as their HCF.

4. Find the value of q. $\sqrt[2]{2^n} = 16$, then $n = $ ____

5. If $64X\,56 - \sqrt[3]{q} = 128X\,24$

6. 15 men, 18 women and 12 boys working together earned Rs 2070. If the daily wages of a man, a woman and a boy are in the ratio 4 : 3 : 2, the daily wages (in Rs) of 1 man, 2 women and 3 boys are ___________.

7. Bolton started business investing Rs 8000. Three months later John joined him investing Rs 6000. If they make a profit of Rs 5100 at the end of the year, how much should be John's share ?

8. The employer reduces the number of employees in the ratio 9 : 8 and increases their wages in the ratio 14 : 15. If the previous wage bill was Rs 189000, what is the amount by which the new wage bill will increase or decrease ?

9. Rs 2010 are to be divided among A, B and C in such a way that if A gets Rs 5, than B must get Rs 12 and if B gets Rs 4, then C must get Rs 5.50. The share of C will exceed that of B by __________.

10. Find the ratio of 12% 0f 12 and 15% of 15.

11. What least number must be added to 1968 to make it divisible by 11?

12. A bottle is full of spirit. One-third of it is taken out and then an equal amount of water is poured into the bottle to fill it. This operation is done four times. Find the final ratio of spirit and water in the bottle.

13. The students in three classes are in the ratio 2 : 3 : 5. If 40 students are increased in each class, the ratio changes to 4 : 5 : 7. Originally the total number of students was _____________.

14. Find the least number which when divided by 12, 24, 36 and 40 leaves a remainder 1, but when divided by 7 leaves no remainder.

15. A drum contains 20 l of a paint. From this, 2 l of paint is taken out and replaced by 2 l of oil. Again 2 l of this mixture is taken out and replaced by 2 l of oil. If this operation is performed once again, then what would be the final ratio of paint and oil in the drum ?

16. 100 ml 80% alcohol and 150 ml 90% alcohol mixed up properly to make a new combination having strength _______ %.

17. Concentrations of three solutions A, B and C are 20%, 30% and 40% respectively. They are mixed in the ratio 3 : 5 : x resulting in a solution of 30% concentration. Find x.

18. Ratio of incomes of A, B and C last year was 3 : 4 : 5. The ratios of their individual incomes of last year and this year are 4 : 5, 2 : 3 and 3 : 4 respectively. If the sum of their present incomes is Rs 78800. Find the present individual income of B.

19. Ravi earns 25% more than Nisha, gut his earning is 18% less than that of Faquir. Find the ratio of their earnings.

20. The cost of manufacturing a TV set is made up of material costs, labour costs and overhead costs. These costs are in the ratio 4 : 3 : 2. If materials costs and labour costs rise by 10% and 8% respectively, while the overhead costs reduce by 5%, what is the percentage increase in the total cost of the TV set ?

21. A number is increased by 20% and then again by 20%. By what per cent should the increased number be reduced so as to get back the original number ?

22. The number of employees working in a farm is increased by 25% and the wages per head are decreased by 25%. If it results in x% decrease in total wages, then the value of x is ___________.

23. A candidate who gets 20% marks in an examination fails by 30 marks but another candidate who gets 32%, gets 42 marks more than the pass marks. The percentage of pass marks is __________.

24. In the expression xy2 , the values of both variables x and y are decreased by 20%. By this the value of the expression will be decreased by ___________________.

25. In an examination Nancy obtained 20% more marks than Hary but are 10% less than Della. If the marks obtained by Hary are 1080, find the percentage of marks obtained by Nancy, if the full marks are 2000.

26. A student took five papers in an examination, where the full marks were the same for each papers, this marks in these papers were in the proportion 6 : 7 : 8 : 9 : 10. In all the papers together, the candidate obtained 60% of the total marks. Then, the number of papers in which he got more than 50% marks is equal to ___________________.

27. A tax payer is exempted of income tax for the first Rs 100000 of his annual income but for the rest of the income, he has to pay a tax at the rate of 20%. If he paid Rs 3160 as income tax for a year, his monthly income is ___________________

28. A house-owner was having his house painted. He was advised that he would require 25 kg of paint. Allowing for 15% wastage and assuming that the paint is available in 2 kg cans, what would be the cost of paint purchased, if one can costs $ 2 ?

29. By receiving 5% less vote than the winner of a by-election a candidate received only 12% of the total vote. Find the ration of votes received by both the candidate.

30. In an election, 10% of the people in the voter's list did not participate. 60 votes were declared invalid. There are only two candidates A and B. A defeated B by 308 votes. It has found that 47% of the people listed in the voters' list voted for A. Find the total number of votes polled.

31. Prices register an increase of 10% on food grains and 15% on other items of expenditure. If the ratio of an employee's expenditure on food grains and other items be 2 : 5, by how much should his salary be increased in order that he may maintain the same level of consumption as before, his present salary being Rs 2590.

32. What is the least number which when divided by the numbers 3, 5, 6, 8, 10 and 12 leaves in each case a remainder 2, but when divided by 13 leaves no remainder.

33. Find the value of p. $144 X\ 36\ -\ \sqrt[3]{p}\ =\ 72 X\ 48$

34. What fraction of a fortnight is an hour?

35. Half a cup sugar measures 130 g. There are ____________ cups of sugar in 5.2 kg pack of sugar.

36. Here m = _____

$$\sqrt[4]{\sqrt[5]{\sqrt[6]{p^8}}}\ =\ p^m$$

37. Prices register an increase of 10% on food grains and 15% on other items of expenditure. If the ratio of an employee's expenditure on food grains and other items be 2 : 5, by how much should his salary be increased in order that he may maintain the same level of consumption as before, his present salary being Rs 2590.

Model Paper XX

1. What per cent is the least rational number of the greatest rational number, if $\frac{11}{12}, \frac{2}{3}, \frac{3}{4}, \frac{5}{9}$ and $\frac{17}{18}$ are arranged in ascending order ?

2. If $\frac{1}{891}$ = 0.00112233445566778899...

   Then what is the value of $\frac{198}{891}$?

3. If $\frac{p}{q}$ = 2.525252525 … …

   then find the value of $\frac{p^2 + q^2}{pq}$.

4. A flower garden is 22.50 m long. Sheela wants to make a border along one side using bricks that are 0.25 m long. How many bricks will be needed?

5. The time taken by Rohan in five different races to run a distance of 500 m was 3.20 minutes, 3.37 minutes, 3.29 minutes, 3.17 minutes and 3.32 minutes. Find the average time taken by him in the races.

6. Anuradha can do a piece of work in 6 hours. What part of the work can she do in 1 hour, in 5 hours, in 6 hours?

7. Ravi can do half of a work alone in 12 days, Munish can do quarter of the same work in 18 days and Roushan can complete one tenth of the work in 2 days. If they all join hands to complete the same work then by what time the entire work will be finished?

8. What is the ratio of two numbers whose difference is 45, and the quotient of the greater number by the lesser number is 4 ?

9. Raj travels 360 km on three fifths of his petrol tank. How far would he travel at the same rate with a full tank of petrol?

10. It takes 17 full specific type of trees to make one tonne of paper. If there are 221 such trees in a forest, then what fraction of forest will be used to make; (a) 5 tonnes of paper. (b) 10 tonnes of paper? To save 7/13th part of the forest how much of paper we have to save?

11. Find the value of $\dfrac{p+1}{p-1} - \dfrac{p-1}{p+1}$,

if $p = \left(1 - \frac{1}{2}\right)\left(1 - \frac{1}{3}\right)\dots\left(1 - \frac{1}{100}\right)$

12. Fractions obtained on multiplying or dividing both numerator and denominator of a given fraction by the same non-zero number, and the given fraction are called ________________ fractions.

13. Find the value of $\left(1 + \frac{1}{2}\right)\left(1 + \frac{1}{3}\right)\dots\dots\left(1 + \frac{1}{1560}\right)$

14. Find the value of p, if
$$p = \frac{0.2 \times 0.14 + 0.5 \times 0.91}{0.1 \times 0.2}$$

15. If $\dfrac{2}{1 + \dfrac{1}{1 + \dfrac{x}{1-x}}} = 1$, then find the value of $\dfrac{x+1}{x-1}$?

16. If x % of 16 = y % of 24, then find the

value of $\dfrac{(x^2 - y^2)}{xy}$

17. If 1.5x = 0.04y then what is the value of $\dfrac{(y-x)}{(y+x)}$?

18. Find the value of p, if $p = \dfrac{(6.4)^2 - (5.4)^2}{8.9^2 + 8.9 \times 2.2 + 1.1^2}$

19. Arrange in ascending order:

$$\sqrt{1.44}, \qquad 8^{\frac{1}{3}}, \qquad \sqrt[3]{0.027},$$
$$0.07 + \sqrt[2]{0.16}, \qquad \sqrt{3^2 + 4^2}$$

20. 13 hundredths is _____ % of 2.6.

21. $\dfrac{17}{15} X \dfrac{17}{15} + \dfrac{2}{15} X \dfrac{2}{15} - \dfrac{17}{15} X \dfrac{4}{15} = $ __________.

22. Find the value of $p^2 + p + 1$, if $p = \dfrac{\left(\left(3\frac{1}{4}\right)^4 - \left(4\frac{1}{3}\right)^4\right)}{\left(3\frac{1}{4}\right)^2 - \left(4\frac{1}{3}\right)^2}$

23. 23% of a number is equal to the thousandth multiple of 92. Find three fifth of that number.

24. All the multiples of 9 are also multiples of _______, but all the multiples of ______ are not necessarily a multiple of 9.

25. Sum total of digits of ones and hundreds place is equal to the digit located at tens place. Number formed by last two digits is a greatest possible multiple of 4. Find the reciprocal of that number.

26. Municipal Corporation of a city has decided to organize plantation works beside a 25 km long road by placing trees beside both the sides of the road at an interval of 50 m. find the total number of trees that can be planted. Also find the cost of maintaining those plants at a rate of $ 2 for every 5 plants.

27. Half of a quarter of 98 = ______.

28. Three bells toll at an interval of 12 seconds, 36 seconds and 45 seconds. After what time interval do they toll together? How many times do they toll together in a gap of three hours?

29. A train moving with a uniform speed of 72 km/h took 2.5 minutes to cross a light post. Find the time taken by it to cross a 1.8 km long platform.

30. Find the value of $\sqrt{272^2 - 128^2}$

31. The square root of 0.4444…. is ____________.

32. 4320 X p is a perfect cube value. Find the value of $p^2 + 3p + 9$

33. $\sqrt[3]{4\frac{12}{125}}$ = x. Find the value of $3x^2 + 4x + 5$

34. $x^3 - 2mx\,2 + 16$ is divisible by x + 2. Find the value of m.

35. $2x^4 - px^3 + 3x^2 + 3x - 2$ is exactly divisible by $x^2 - 3x + 2$. Find the value of $p^2 + 3p + 17$.

36. Find the following:

$$64^a = \frac{1}{256^b},$$

i) $3a + 4b = $ _________

ii) $\dfrac{(a+b)}{ab} = $ _________

37. Complete the following:

$$6^x - 6^{x-3} = 7740 ; \quad x^x$$

38. Find the value of $p^2 + 8p + 21$

$$p = \left(2^{\frac{1}{4}} - 1\right)\left(2^{\frac{3}{4}} + 2^{\frac{1}{2}} + 2^{\frac{1}{4}} + 1\right) = $$ _________

39. Find the value of p.

$$a = (\sqrt{3} + \sqrt{2})^{-3}, \quad b$$
$$= (\sqrt{3} - \sqrt{2})^{-3},$$
$$p = [(a+1)^{-1} + (b+1)^{-1}]$$

40.   Half a dozen banana costs \$ 12. Find the cost of 20 bananas.

41. Arrange in ascending $16^{\frac{1}{2}}, \sqrt[4]{16}, \sqrt[2]{81}, \sqrt[3]{125}$ order.

42. Some bananas are to be shared among a number of children. To give each child 9 bananas would require 15 more bananas. But if the share of each is 8 there are 10 bananas left over. How many bananas are there?

43. In a number of three digits the units digit is double the tens' digit. The sum of the number and the number formed by reversing the digits is 1191 and the average of three digits is 5. What is the number?

44. Ten percent of 29 is ______ less than 5% of 300.

45. A sold a watch to B at 20% gain and B sold it to C at a loss of 10%. If C bought the watch for Rs 216, at what price did A purchase it ?

46. A man sold two steel chairs for Rs 500 each. On one, he gains 20% and on the other he loss 12%. How much does he gain or loss in the whole transaction ?

Model Paper XXI

1. $P = 515.15 - 15.51 - 1.51 - 5.11 - 1.11$.
   Find the value of $2P + 1$

2. If $a = (7.5 \times 7.5 + 37.5 + 2.5 \times 2.5)$, then find the value of $\dfrac{a^2+1}{a^2-1} - \dfrac{a^2-1}{a^2+1}$

3. A began a business with Rs 45000 and B joined after wards with Rs 30000. At the end of a year, the profit is divided in the ratio 2:1. When did B join ?

4. An employer reduces the number of his employees in the ratio 7: 5 and increases their wages in the ratio 15 : 28. State whether his bill of total wages increase or decrease and in what ratio.

5. In three vessels, the ratio of water and milk is 6 : 7, 5 : 9 and 8 : 7 respectively. If the mixtures of the three vessels are mixed together, then what will be the ratio of water and milk ?

6. A drum contains 20 liters of a paint. From this, 2 liters of paint is taken out and replaced by 2 liters of oil. Again 2 liters of this mixture is taken out and replaced by 2 liters of oil. If this operation is performed once again, then what would be the final ratio of paint and oil in the drum ?

7. If $a : (b + c) = 1 : 3$ and $c : (a + b) = 5 : 7$, then $b : (a + c) = $ ___ .

8. 15 men, 18 women and 12 boys working together earned Rs 2070. If the daily wages of a man, a woman and a boy are in the ratio 4 : 3 : 2, the daily wages (in Rs) of 1 man, 2 women and 3 boys are ________________ .

9. Ratio of the incomes of A, B and C last year was 3 : 4 : 5. The ratio of their individual incomes during the last year and this year are 4 : 5, 2 : 3 and 3 : 4 respectively. If the sum of their present incomes is Rs 78800, then find the present individual income of A, B and C.

10. 10% of A = 20% of B = 30% of C. Find the value $\dfrac{AB+BC+AC}{ABC}$.

11. $\dfrac{1}{10}$ of a number x exceeds $\dfrac{1}{15}$ of another number y by 5. Find the value of P.

$$P = \frac{3x-2y}{3x+2y} + \frac{3x+2y}{3x-2y} .$$

12. Tap A can fill a tank in 30 minutes and tap B can fill the same tank in 40 minutes. Both the tap can fill the tank jointly in _____ mins.

13. In two alloys, copper and zinc are related in the ratio of 4 : 1 and 1 : 3. 10 kg of 1st alloy, 16 kg of 2nd alloy and some of pure copper are melted together. An alloy was obtained in which the ratio of copper to zinc was 3 : 2. Find the weight of the new alloy ?

14. Railway fares of 1st, 2nd and 3rd classes between two stations were in the ratio 8 : 6 : 3. The fares of 1st and 2nd class were subsequently reduced by $\frac{1}{6}$ and $\frac{1}{12}$ respectively. If during a year, the ratio between the passengers of 1st, 2nd and 3rd classes was 9 : 12 : 26 and the total amount collected by the sale of tickets was Rs 1088, the collection from the passengers of 1st class was ______________.

15. Salary of Mark is increased by 16%. His previous salary was _____ % less than that of the increased salary.

16. Solve the following equation : $\frac{11}{144} X \frac{12}{169} X \frac{13}{121} X \frac{132}{341} X \frac{682}{1001} X \frac{13}{19} =$

17. What least number must added to the smallest six digit number and must be subtracted from the largest five digit number to make both of them a multiple of 11?

18. What least number must be added to 121.098 to make it a multiple of 1.001?

19. First tap can fill a water tank in 30 minutes and second tap can empty the half filled tank in 1.5 hours. By what time the empty tank will be filled up if both the tap kept open?

20. Half of a cake is given to all friends, half of the remaining portion of the cake retained by parents, one third of what remaining was distributed amongst John's classmates. Finally John received only 200 g of the cake. Find the quantity of that cake.

21. Three items are purchased at $ 450 each. One of them is sold at a loss of 10%. At what price should the other two be sold so as to gain 20% on the whole transaction? What is the gain% on these two items?

22. A boat covers 30 km in 3 hours in the direction of a stream. It covers the same distance in opposite direction of the stream. Find speed of the boat in still water.

[Ans: 8 km/h]

23. Find the least number located in between 454003 and 354302 which is a multiple of 209. Also find other two factors.

Model Paper XXII

1. Find the digit present in the thousands place in the product
    a. $(11011 \div 11)$ X 7,000 = _____________
    b. $(121 \div 11)$ X 8,000 = _____________
    c. $(12310 \div 11)$ X 9,000 = _____________
    d. $(12221 \div 121)$ X 6,000 = _____________

2. Sum total of the smallest and the greatest four digit numbers formed by without repeating any digits twice is _____________ more than the smallest five digit number.

3. 9,876 + 1,023 = _________________.

4. 3. Difference of digits of a two digit number is 7. if digits are reversed then sum total of both the number becomes the predecessor of the three digit smallest number. Find the second multiple of this number.

5. 4. Compare the place value of 3 in 2,309 and 3,283. Find the difference of both the place values of 3. The difference is the _(____) th multiple of 100.

6. 121, 169 and 219 have following things in common:
    I. All these numbers are square numbers.
    II. These are square numbers of odd primes.
    III. These numbers have equal numbers of   prime factors.
    Select which of the statements mentioned above are true.
    A: Only I   B: Only II   C: Both I and III   D: All I, II and III

7. Complete the Prime factorisation:
    a) 141   = ______   X___;
    b) 84 = _________________;
    c) 363 = __________ X ___________ ;
    d) 3,000 = 2 X 2 X 2 X _________________
    e) 729 = __ X __X___ X ___X___;
    f) __________ = 89 X 11

8. In the calculation table depicted below numbers are related to each other. Find their inter relations and also identify missing numbers.

9. 32 X 10,000 = ___________ X 16 = _________ X 8.

10. 8th multiple of 16 is _______________ multiple of 32.

11. 9th multiple of 11 is ________ multiple of 9.

12. After subtracting ____________ we can obtain 3rd multiple of 13 from the 4th multiple of 1

    a. Complete the following: 1, 4, 9, __a___, __b___, ___c___;

b) a X b + c = ________________

c) 1, 8, 27, ________, ___________ , _______________ .

d) 121, ________, ___________ , _____________ 161.

e) 64, ________, _______ , ________ , 16, 9.

13. Some of the statements regarding prime and composite numbers are given below.

    I : 1 is not a prime **or** composite number.

    II : Two is the only even prime number.

    III: All odd numbers are not prime.

    IV: All composite numbers can be written as product of prime numbers.

    V: 101 has only two factors 1 and the number itself. That is why it is a prime number

    Which of the above statements are true?

    A: Only I   B: All   C: I, II and III D: Only II, III and IV

14. Product of all the factors of 6 = __________

A: 36   B: 12   C: 18   D: 24

15.. Complete the following:

    a. A number that consists of a whole number and a fraction is called a/an ____________?

    b. An_____________________ is a number that represents a part of a whole.

    c. A fraction whose numerical (absolute) value is greater than 1 is called a/an _______________, and a fraction whose numerical value is between 0 and 1 is called a/an ______________.

    d. ______________ mean the same value.

    e. The product of two proper fractions is ________ than each of the fractions that are multiplied.

    f. While dividing a fraction by another fraction, we __________ the first fraction by the ________ of the other fraction.

g. $52.7 \div$ ________ $= 0.527$

h. 0.5 _____ $0.7 = 0.35$

    i. $2.001 \div 0.003 =$ __________   ii. $3.0402 \div 0.027 =$ __________ .

16. The H.C.F. of two numbers is 42 and their L.C.M. is 1260. If one of the numbers is 210, find the other?

17. Is there any pair of number having HCF 13 and LCM 121?

18. Calculate the least number which when divided by 35, 45, 55, leaves remainders 18, 28 and 38 respectively.

19. Two numbers are in the ratio of 13 : 15 and their L.C.M. is 39780. Then the numbers are?

20. Three numbers which are co-prime to each other are such that the product of the first two is 551 and that of the last two is 1073. The sum of the three numbers is__________.

[Middle number will be H.C.F. of two terminal numbers.]

21. _______________ will divide 400, 435 and 541 leaving 9, 10 and 14 as remainders, respectively.

22. Three athletes completed their rounds in 18 seconds, 24 seconds and 44 seconds, respectively. After how many seconds will they be together at the starting point?

23. Arrange in ascending and descending order .

12.12, 28.7%, 121 hundredths, (21 + 0.21 + 1.012), 21% of 60

24. What least number must be added to 132.98 to make it divisible by 8?

25. Simplify: $6\frac{2}{9} + 2\frac{7}{9} - 4\frac{3}{11} + 1\frac{3}{11}$

26. 25% of 80 =

27. Simplify : $78 - [5 + 3 \text{ of } (25 - 2 \times 10)]$

28. Simplify : $78 - [24 - 16 - \{5 - (4 - 1)\}]$

29. $\sqrt{a} = 9$; $Find\ the\ value\ of\ \frac{a+1}{a-1} - \frac{a-1}{a+1}$

30. $\frac{21}{39} \ X \frac{78}{63} \ X \frac{39}{49} \ X \frac{63}{13} \ X \frac{121}{270} =$

31. In each of the following series some of the square numbers are missing. Try to find them out.

    a.   841, ?, 2401, 3481, 4761

    b.   1, 9, 25, ?, 81, 121

    c.   625, ______, 225, 100, 25

    d.   729, 6859, 24389, ?, 117649, 205379

Model Paper XXIII

1. Rohit had a candy bar divided into 16 equal parts. He gave 3 pieces to Kamalika and 2 pieces to Mohan. What fraction of Candy bar is left with him?

2. Mohan added 43 tens and 387 hundreds to get a five digit number which is __________ less than the six digit smallest number.

3. How many faces are there in the following shape?

4. There are ______ curved face(s) and _____ flat faces in a solid cylinder.

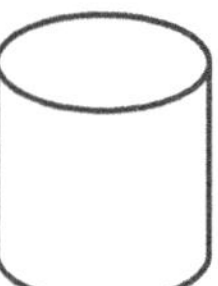

5. Mohan reached his office by 15 minutes late. It was 11:28 A.M. What was his office time?

6. While calculating perimeter of her garden Ratna calculated the length and breadth of the garden. It was 1500 m long and 600 m wide. _____ times the sum total of length and __________ will be the perimeter of the garden. Find the perimeter in km.

7. For a punch bowl, Carin needs a block of ice with a volume of at least 125 cubic inches. She has a cube of ice that is five inches on each side. Write the volume of the cube using a base and exponents. Then write it in standard form. Is the block of ice big enough? Remember that volume is calculated by multiplying length times width times height.

8. Tickets to the school play cost Rs 300 for adults and Rs 200 for students. If 235 adults and 322 students attended the play, write an expression that shows the total amount of money made on ticket sales. Then simplify the expression.

9. During vacation you spent Rs 127 out of Rs 250. There was another 500 rupees note with you. Find the money left with you.

10. The Akshi Kaikyo suspension bridge in Japan has a span of 6,570 feet. The Humber suspension bridge in England has a span of 4,626 feet. How much longer is the Humber suspension bridge than the Akshi Kaikyo suspension bridge?

11. Julio increases the laps he runs by three laps each day. If he begins on Monday running 4 laps, how many laps will he run on Wednesday at his current rate?

12. Adam is starting a business to take people on hot-air balloon rides. He knows that to carry 2 people, the balloon must have a volume of about 60,000 cubic feet. For his business, he wants a balloon that will carry 4 people. He calculates that the balloon must have a volume of 120,000 cubic feet. Is his answer reasonable? Explain.

13. __________ is the only natural number having only one factor.

14. A ___________ has no end point, a ______ has only one end point and a _______ ____________ has two endpoints.

15. A circular wire is reshaped to form a square of 20 cm side. What was the circumference of that circle?

16. Find the difference of areas of two squares having sides 30 cm and 40 cm respectively.

17. A swimming pool measures 50 m by 20 m. The manager plans to construct a cemented road around the pool, which should measure 4 m wide. What is the area of the cemented road?

18. A triangle having more than one ________ angle or more than one ________ angle is not possible.

19. A regular heptagon has _____ lines of symmetry.

20. A hexagon having only one lines of _______ is possible.

21. $5 \times 39 = 5 \times ($ __________ + _____ $)$

22. A solid cylinder has ______ curved face(s) and _______ flat face(s).

23. A sphere has _______ curved face(s) and _______ flat faces.

24. __________ is a four digit greatest number divisible by 4 and 3.

25.

Model Paper XXIV

1. Complete the following number pattern:
a) 88,_______, __________, __________, 33, __________. __________.
b) 121, _________, __________, _________, ______, 55, _____, ________, 22, 11
c) 12, ____, _______, 12,345, _______________.
d) 10204, ______, ___________, _______________, ____________ , 12,204, 12,404.
e) 144, ______, ___________, _______________, 96, 84 , ________, _______.
2. Add : MMDCXX + MCDXCLVI
3. Subtract: MMMCLX – MCMLXXXV
4. Arrange the following in ascending and descending order:
a) MDC, MCMLXV, MCDXCLV, MDLXVIII
b) XXII, XXXVIII, XCLXXVI, XVI
c) MMMCMXCIX, MMMXII, MMMCMXXII,
5. Compare:
a) MMMCMXCIX ______ MMMDCXCIX;
b) CMCCX _________ MCCX
c) XXIV _______XXXIII
6. Complete the following:
   36,653   = _____   + ___ + _____ +___ + _______.
7. 2,892   =   X 1000 + …. X 100   + …. X 10   + …….X 1
8. Complete the following:
a) _____________ are what we can multiply to get numbers.
b) _____________ are what we get after multiplying the number by any other number.
c) _____________ is a factor of all the numbers.
d) All the numbers are one of the multiple of _____________.
e) All _____________ numbers have only two factors, 1 and the number itself.
f) 36 has _____________ factors in all.
g) 36 has _____________ prime factors in all.
h) All the factors of 18 are also _____________ of 36, but all the _____________ of 36 are not the factors of 18.
i) _____________ are always greater than or equal to the number.
9. Multiples of 4 are also multiples of 2, but all multiples of 2 are not necessarily multiples of _____________.
10. _____________ is the smallest three digit number divisible by 8.

11: Estimation: ….

Choose the best estimated difference.

1. 0.89 − 0.22   a. 0.7   b. 0.8   c. 0.5   d. 0.9

2. 18.19 − 7.23   a. 12   b. 9   c. 11   d. 8

3. 0.506 − 0.38   a. 0.1   b. 0.3   c. 0.4   d. 0.5

Estimate the difference by rounding.

4. 0.73 − 0.4

5. 7.3 − 2.16

6. 0.582 − 0.43

7. 5.879 − 3.71

8. 26.259 − 13.4

9. 0.476 − 0.32   10. 14.8 − 9.223   11. 50.78 − 9.6

Estimate the difference. Use front-end estimation.

12. 0.87 − 0.4

13. 0.695 − 0.26

14. 9.347 − 8.12

15. 23.754 − 12.412

13: Complete the following.

1. Put a tick ✔ in the box for the shape that is divided into equal parts.

(a) 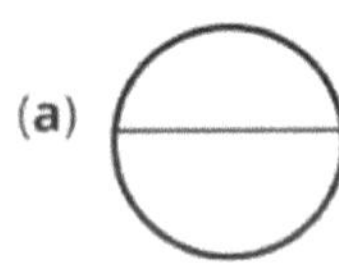 (b) 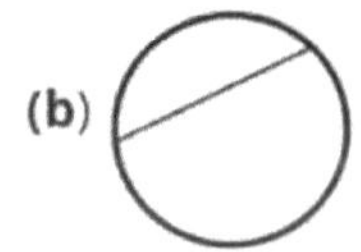 (c) 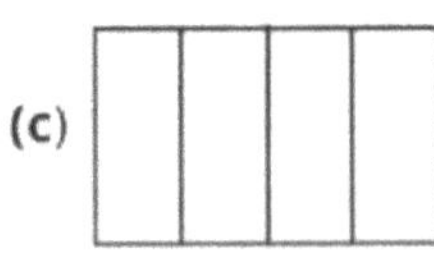 (d) 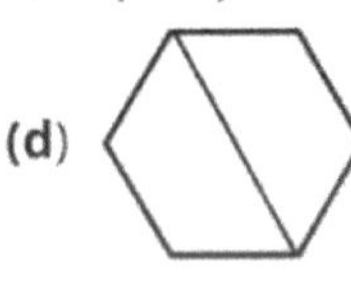 (e) 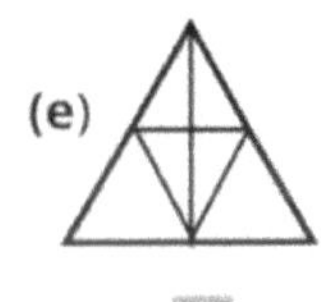

2. Circle the shapes that are divided into halves.

(a) 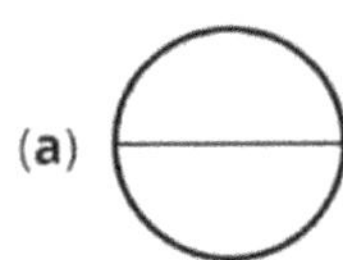 (b) 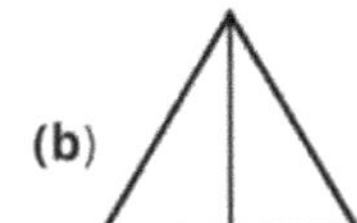 (c)  (d) 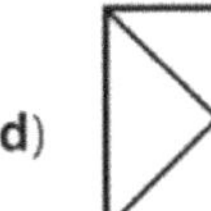 (e) 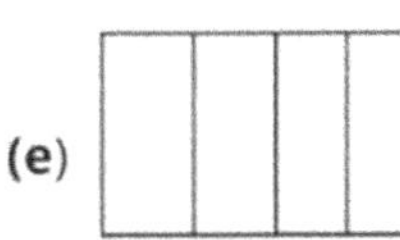

3. what fraction of each figure is colored. Write their numerator and denminator as well.

(a) 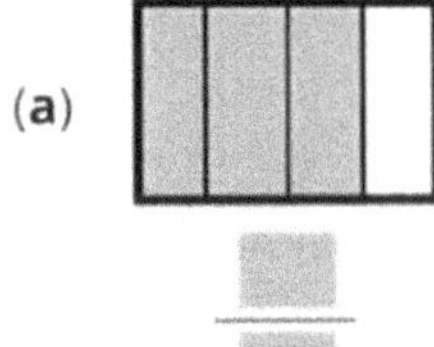 (b) 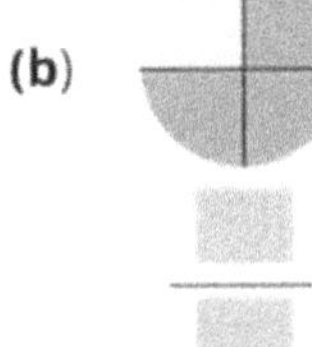 (c) 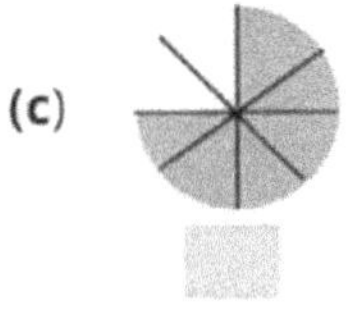 (d) 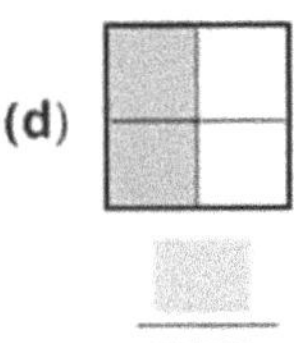

Model Paper XXV

In the number 308,610,547,823, write the digit in the:

1. ten-billions place 2. millions place 3. hundred-thousands place

Write the number in standard form.

4. three hundred four billion, six hundred thousand 5. CCLXI

6. 1,000,000,000 + 40,000 + 80 + 3 7. eight and twelve thousandths

Write the word name for each number.

8. 360,071 9. 1,009,124,008 10. 6.71 11. 0.531 12. CMLXI

Compare. Write <, =, or >.

13. 185,035,013 _?_ 185,503,013 14. 10.09 _?_ 10.1 15. 9.63 _?_ 9.630

Write in order from least to greatest.

16. 6,135,936; 6,315,396; 6,531,639; 6,153,693 17. 3.12; 31.2; 0.312

Round each number to the place of the underlined digit.

18. 474,19<u>8</u>,575 19. <u>3</u>13,983,156 20. 145.<u>7</u>28 21. $766.<u>1</u>3

Find the missing addend.

22. 8 + □ = 15 23. □ + 9 = 17 24. 14 = □ + 7 25. 11 = 6 + □

Use rounding to estimate. Then add or subtract.

26.		27.		28.		29.		30.	
	25,736		503,149		$235.17		600,000		$907.15
	12,548		180,590		137.23		−421,351		− 35.43
	+36,985		+248,762		+ 427.45				

27. Find the smallest number which can be subtracted from the greatest number of five digits to make the number divisible by 11.

28. Add: 0.1 + 1.001 + 11.101 + 101.11011 = ...

29. Half of a quarter of 16,016 = ...

30. What fraction of all the numbers from 1 to 20 are prime numbers?

31. What fraction of all the numbers starting from 1 to 200 are multiples of 25?

Model Paper XXVI

Use the diagram to complete each statement.

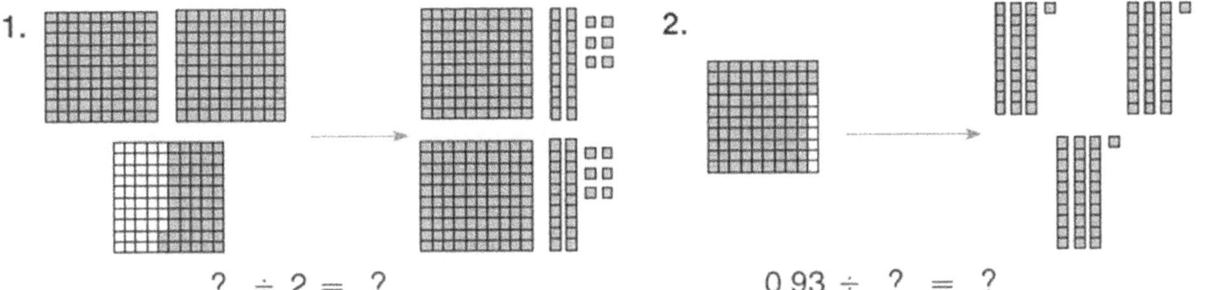

1. $\underline{\ ?\ } \div 2 = \underline{\ ?\ }$

2. $0.93 \div \underline{\ ?\ } = \underline{\ ?\ }$

Divide and check.

3. $8\overline{)5.6}$ 4. $9\overline{)5.4}$ 5. $6\overline{)0.96}$ 6. $5\overline{)0.75}$ 7. $4\overline{)0.76}$

8. $4\overline{)0.924}$ 9. $9\overline{)2.214}$ 10. $4\overline{)25.72}$ 11. $3\overline{)\$0.84}$ 12. $6\overline{)\$55.56}$

13. $76.8 \div 8$ 14. $9.513 \div 7$ 15. $\$364.50 \div 5$ 16. $\$346.32 \div 9$

Find the quotient.

17. $n \div 5$ when $n = 2.5$ 18. $n \div 3$ when $n = 0.63$

19. $0.861 \div n$ when $n = 7$ 20. $41.36 \div n$ when $n = 8$

Compare. Write <, =, or >.

21. $1.2 \div 3 \ \underline{\ ?\ }\ 0.84 \div 2$ 22. $31.92 \div 4 \ \underline{\ ?\ }\ 23.55 \div 5$

23. $0.8 \div 2 \ \underline{\ ?\ }\ \frac{4}{5} \div 2$ 24. $2.4 \div 6 \ \underline{\ ?\ }\ \frac{3}{4} \div 3$

25. A large bag holds 24.9 lb. This is 3 times the weight a small bag holds. How much does a small bag hold?

26. Mr. Lee drove 232.5 km in 5 days. If he drove the same distance each day, what distance did he drive in one day?

Use a number line to complete each division sentence.

27. $2 \div 0.4 = n$

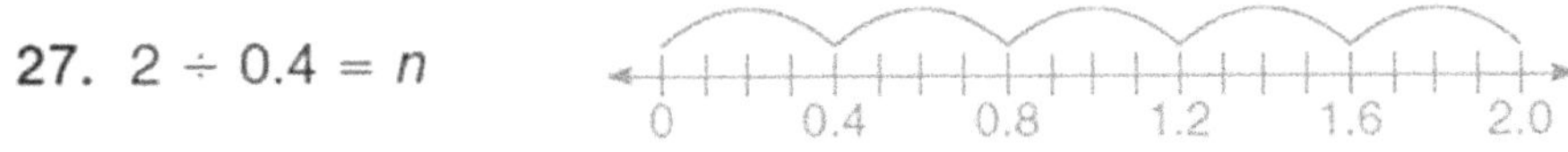

28. $6 \div 0.5 = n$ 29. $4 \div 0.8 = n$ 30. $7 \div 0.2 = n$

31. $4.5 \div 0.3 = n$ 32. $3.6 \div 0.9 = n$ 33. $4.2 \div 0.7 = n$

34. Sum total of digits of a three digit number is a multiple of 5. The digit placed in the middle is the sum total of other two digits. Find all such possible numbers. Also find their sum total.

35. Hour hand of a wall mount clock makes ________ angles at the centre while rotating throughout the day,

Model Paper XXVII

Write the decimal point in the product.
Write in zeros where necessary.

1.	0.3 × 0.2 —— 6	2.	0.0 4 × 0.3 ——— 1 2	3.	0.3 4 × 0.2 ——— 6 8	4.	7.4 × 0.0 1 ——— 7 4	5.	0.0 0 8 × 7 ——— 5 6

Multiply.

6.	0.2 × 0.1	7.	0.04 × 0.2	8.	0.03 × 9	9.	0.003 × 3	10.	0.002 × 4

11.	0.16 × 0.3	12.	0.46 × 0.2	13.	0.19 × 0.4	14.	0.012 × 3	15.	0.021 × 4

16.	1.3 × 0.03	17.	1.1 × 0.05	18.	2.3 × 0.04	19.	6.7 × 0.01	20.	1.7 × 0.04

Find the product.

21. 3.2×0.02 22. 0.7×0.02 23. 5.2×0.01 24. 0.13×0.3

25. 2×0.021 26. 0.3×0.11 27. 0.5×0.05 28. 1.2×0.04

29. $n \times 0.006$ when $n = 8$ 30. $n \times 0.4$ when $n = 0.05$

31. $0.3 \times n$ when $n = 0.07$ 32. $0.04 \times n$ when $n = 1.9$

Compute. Use the order of operations.

33. $0.35 \times (3 - 0.5)$ 34. $(0.09 \times 0.8) + (0.3 \times 0.6)$

35. $1.8 - 0.3 \times 0.02 + 0.9$ 36. $(0.28 + 3.2) \times 0.4$

37. A clock uses 0.02 kilowatt hours of electricity a day. How much electricity does it use in 4 days?

38. A postcard weighs 0.004 kg. How many kilograms would six of these weigh?

39. Cocoa hulls make up 0.08 of Jamal's organic fertilizer mix. Teresa uses nine tenths of that amount in her mix. What portion of Teresa's mix is cocoa hulls?

40. A radio uses three 1.5-volt batteries. It stops playing if the batteries lose two hundredths of their total power. What is the minimum voltage the radio needs?

41. A train is moving with a uniform speed of 12 m per second. It takes 40 seconds to cross a telephone post. The train is _______ m long.

Model Paper XXVIII

Write the place of the underlined digit. Then write its value.

1. 131,241,920,057

2. 670,901,230,001,400

3. 80,270,310,000

4. 0.4297

5. 0.81523

6. 7.014325

7. 106.1876

8. 177.92743

9. 60.197608

Use the number 64,310,420,069,346.789125. Name the digit in the given place.

10. millions

11. ten trillions

12. hundred billions

13. trillions

14. millionths

15. hundredths

16. tenths

17. ten thousandths

18. hundred thousandths

Write the word name for each number.

19. 201,000,006,400

20. 20,030,010,000

21. 6,000,121,000,015

22. 210.004

23. 198.0408

24. 1,210.00062

25. 1,010.000079

26. 105.042019

27. 201.568970

Write each of the following number in standard form.

28. thirteen million, five thousand

29. three hundred eight billion

30. one hundred twelve trillion

31. ninety-one billion, fifty

32. eleven millionths, 23 hundreds

33. two thousand ten hundred thousandths

34. 750 trillion, eight billion

35. 42 ten thousandths

Write each of the following in expanded form in two ways.

36. 5,042,102

37. 201,407,090,000

38. 15,000,087,000

39. 1.210.045678

40. 12.203.050904

41. 1.078.500901

42. 14 tens + 14 hundreds + 14 thousandths + 14 thousands + 14 hundredths + 14

43. One fifth of fifteenth multiple of greatest five digit odd number increased by 15,000

44. 95 trillion, 700 million

45. 8 trillion, twelve million, five

46. 13 billion, 7 hundred

47. 14 hundred thousandths

48. 80 and 13 ten thousandths

49. 907 millionths

50. 29 tens + 209 tenths + 2,009 thousandths + 209,209 + 209 hundredths

Model Paper XXIX

Write each power of ten in standard form.

1. 10^8 **2.** 10^2 **3.** 10^{-2} **4.** 10^{-4}

5. 10^{-1} **6.** 10^{-3} **7.** 10^0 **8.** 10^7

Write each as a power of ten.

9. $10 \times 10 \times 10$ **10.** $10 \times 10 \times 10 \times 10 \times 10$ **11.** 10

12. 0.0001   **13.** 0.1   **14.** 0.001

Write each number in expanded form using exponents.

15. 1005   **16.** 218   **17.** 52,905   **18.** 840,500
$(1 \times 10^3) + (5 \times 10^0)$

19. 2.0006   **20.** 9.107   **21.** 77.04   **22.** 7.0034

Write each in standard form.

23. $(5 \times 10^7) + (8 \times 10^3) + (3 \times 10^1)$ **24.** $(1 \times 10^6) + (6 \times 10^3) + (2 \times 10^0)$

Round the following to the nearest cent.

25. $4.368   26. $5.472   27. $35.476   28. $12.525

29. $.463   30. $.085   31. $1.5971   32. $99.9943

Round each number to the underlined place.

33. 94,329   34. 17,721   35. 0.19716   36. 3.14159

37. 2.71828   38. 100.5003   39. 99.59   40. 0.66666

Round each number to the greatest nonzero place.

41. 2.8104   42. 0.609   43. 0.0703   44. 0.00394

45. 68.3047   46. 44.08243   47. 0.0084032   48. 0.004073

49. The average distance from the sun to Earth rounded to the nearest million is about 93,000,000 miles. What is the greatest whole number that the actual distance could be?

50. Light travels at an average speed of 3,00,000 km /s. Light from a star reaches us in 20 minutes and 8 seconds. Calculate distance of that star from the earth. Represent the figure by using scientific notation.

51. Simplify: $[(1.001 + 1.001 + 1.001 \ldots\ldots 3{,}000 \text{ times}) \times 10^{-3}] \div 1{,}001 = \ldots\ldots\ldots$

52. Kathleen has covered 46.75 m in the special race in a minute. About how much farther and with what average speed must she go to complete the 500 m race in 10 minutes?

Model Paper XXX

Compare. Write <, =, or >.

1. 0.46 _?_ 0.39   **2.** 0.709 _?_ 0.921   **3.** 0.06 _?_ 0.60

4. 9.8 _?_ 9.80   **5.** 0.509 _?_ 0.510   **6.** 0.623 _?_ 0.627

7. 0.4286 _?_ 0.4190   **8.** 0.5691 _?_ 0.5690   **9.** 0.53 _?_ 0.536

10. 0.8 _?_ 0.78   **11.** 7.610 _?_ 7.61   **12.** 7.3 _?_ 7.301

13. 2.34 _?_ 2.3513   **14.** 91.42 _?_ 90.425   **15.** 0.059 _?_ 0.59

Write in order from greatest to least.

16. 0.75, 0.39, 0.2, 0.35   **17.** 0.484, 0.495, 0.523, 0.54

18. 8.63, 8.6, 8.65, 7.99   **19.** 9.21, 9.0, 9.2, 9.06

II: Use number line for comaring values…

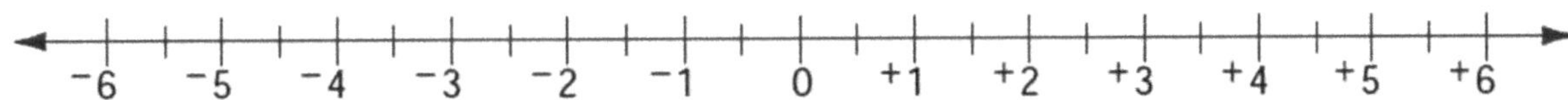

1. $\frac{^-1}{2}$ _?_ $\frac{^-3}{4}$ **2.** $^-0.5$ _?_ $^+0.75$ **3.** $^-3.5$ _?_ $^-4.25$ **4.** $^+3\frac{1}{4}$ _?_ $^+3\frac{1}{8}$

5. $^-4$ _?_ $\frac{^-6}{3}$ **6.** $^+2.5$ _?_ $^-3\frac{1}{2}$ **7.** $^-5\frac{1}{8}$ _?_ $^+4$ **8.** $^-6$ _?_ $^-5.75$

9. 0 _?_ $^-3.25$ **10.** $\frac{^+3}{4}$ _?_ 0   **11.** $\frac{^-8}{2}$ _?_ $^-4$ **12.** $\frac{^-1}{8}$ _?_ $^-0.125$

Write in order from least to greatest. Use the number line above to help.

13. $^-3, ^-4\frac{1}{2}, 2$ **14.** $0, \frac{^-1}{2}, 2\frac{1}{4}$ **15.** $5, 0, \frac{2}{1}$ **16.** $^-4, 3\frac{1}{4}, ^-1.5$

17. $^-2.25, ^+0.25, ^-1.5$ **18.** $^-2\frac{1}{2}, 2.5, ^-1\frac{1}{4}$ **19.** $\frac{1}{4}, \frac{^-1}{4}, 0$ **20.** $5\frac{1}{4}, ^-1, ^-2\frac{3}{4}$

21. $\frac{6}{3}, \frac{^-3}{4}, ^-4$ **22.** $\frac{^-3}{4}, \frac{2}{1}, 1\frac{1}{4}$ **23.** $\frac{3}{2}, ^-2\frac{1}{2}, 3$ **24.** $\frac{^-4}{2}, ^-1.5, ^-2\frac{1}{2}$

25: Which of the following is the greatest? $12^0\,F$, $-32\,^0F$, $108^0\,F$

Model Paper XXXI

Estimate the sum or difference. Use front-end estimation with adjustments.

1. $\begin{array}{r} 31.6 \\ +\,18.1 \end{array}$	**2.** $\begin{array}{r} 68.7 \\ -\,63.9 \end{array}$	**3.** $\begin{array}{r} 7.5 \\ -\,2.9 \end{array}$	**4.** $\begin{array}{r} 9.1 \\ -\,3.6 \end{array}$	**5.** $\begin{array}{r} 0.87 \\ -\,0.54 \end{array}$
6. $\begin{array}{r} 0.74 \\ -\,0.15 \end{array}$	**7.** $\begin{array}{r} 76.67 \\ 23.89 \\ +\,69.47 \end{array}$	**8.** $\begin{array}{r} 16.34 \\ 44.59 \\ +\,39.07 \end{array}$	**9.** $\begin{array}{r} 0.66 \\ 0.7 \\ +\,0.19 \end{array}$	**10.** $\begin{array}{r} 0.84 \\ 0.59 \\ +\,0.8 \end{array}$

Estimate the sum or difference by rounding.

11. $\begin{array}{r} 18.1534 \\ +\ \ 7.0901 \end{array}$	**12.** $\begin{array}{r} 4.8359 \\ -\,0.7473 \end{array}$	**13.** $\begin{array}{r} 0.45601 \\ +\,0.06428 \end{array}$	**14.** $\begin{array}{r} 4371.5902 \\ -\ \ 127.3246 \end{array}$
15. $\begin{array}{r} 386{,}002{,}444 \\ -\ \ 49{,}624{,}973 \end{array}$	**16.** $\begin{array}{r} 2.361912 \\ -\,0.19008 \end{array}$	**17.** $\begin{array}{r} 952.0667 \\ 232.608 \\ +\,351.03991 \end{array}$	**18.** $\begin{array}{r} 7.30267 \\ 45.37 \\ +\ \ 0.84652 \end{array}$

19: In a science experiment duly conducted at school, Smith discovered that his record of the changes in a liquid's temperature formed a definite pattern. In each of the first 3 minutes, the temperature increased 1.5° F; in each of the next 2 minutes, it decreased 0.55° F. Then this pattern repeated itself. If Smith started measuring the temperature at 30° F, how long would it take the temperature scale to reach 82° F?

20: Tunitia caught 12 fish on Monday, 14 on Tuesday, 18 on Wednesday, 26 on Thursday, and so on. Following this definite pattern, how many fish did he catch on Saturday?

21: Mishutka folds a sheet of drawing paper in fourths, then in thirds, and then in half. Estimate into how many parts his paper is divided.

22: Observe the process displayed in the following temperature presentation.

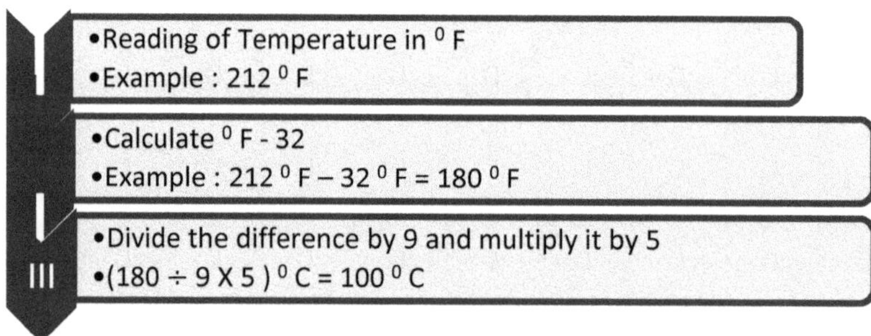

Convert 132⁰ F in Celcius scale.

www.ingramcontent.com/pod-product-compliance
Lightning Source LLC
Chambersburg PA
CBHW042050150726
48005CB00036B/2940